Black Americana

DETROIT PUBLIC LIBRARY
3 5674 02167812 4

D0061907

Step It Down

Bessie Jones and Bess Lomax Hawes

Step It Down

Games, Plays, Songs, and Stories from the Afro-American Heritage

Brown Thrasher Books

The University of Georgia Press *Athens and London*

Published by the University of Georgia Press
Athens, Georgia 30602

The paper in this book meets the guidelines for permanence and durability of the Committee on Production Guidelines for Book Longevity of the Council on Library Resources.

Printed in the United States of America

97 96 95 94 93 P 8 7 6 5

Library of Congress Cataloging in Publication Data

Jones, Bessie, 1902–
Step it down.

Reprint. Originally published: New York: Harper & Row, 1972.
"Brown thrasher books."
Bibliography: p.
Includes index.
1. Afro-Americans—Folklore. 2. Afro-American children's games. 3. Games with music—Southern States. 4. Folk-songs—Southern States. 5. Afro-Americans—Songs and music. I. Hawes, Bess Lomax, 1921– . II. Title.
[GR111.A47J66 1987] 796.1'3 87-5945
ISBN 0-8203-0960-5 (pbk.: alk. paper)

British Library Cataloging in Publication Data available.

Contents

Preface to the Brown Thrasher Edition

As I look back over the original edition of *Step It Down* it seems to me that it should stand as it was written fifteen years ago, especially now that I can no longer consult my co-author. Bessie Smith Jones passed away of leukemia on September 4, 1984. She was eighty-three years old, and her health had been failing for several years.

In the last decade of her life, she had won many honors. She taught for a year at Yale University through a Duke Ellington Fellowship. She performed extensively during the summer-long Bicentennial Festival of American Folklife on the National Mall, and her work in the Children's Program there was videotaped by the Smithsonian Institution. A portion of the numerous interviews she gave throughout her lifetime detailing her reminiscences was published in a book co-authored by John Stewart and titled *For The Ancestors* (University of Illinois Press, 1982); and two additional recordings of her singing with various assemblages of children in eastern schools were released under the titles *So Glad I'm Here* and *Step It Down* (Rounder Records 2015 and 8004). In 1982, she received a National Heritage Fellowship from the National Endowment for the Arts; Mrs. Jones was one of the first eminent folk artists so honored by the United States government.

On hearing of her death, Alan Lomax, who had first recorded her in the 1940s said, "She was on fire to teach America. In my heart, I call her the Mother Courage of American Black traditions." And Professor Willie Ruff, with whom she had worked at Yale, commented, "The woman was a metaphor for the continuity of Black tradition." Her great-niece, Frankie Quimby, put it another way, "Miss Bessie always said she wanted to live on. That's what she wanted, she wanted to live on."

Bessie Smith Jones will live on, of course, in the memories of the thousands of people she touched with the blazing force of her personality. And perhaps the re-issue of *Step It Down* will help keep her alive for generations of children and teachers yet to come. But it must be written somewhere that her work with children and her educational philosophy, complex and detailed as it was, was only a small part of what she had to offer. The songs in this book, for example, are perhaps less than a twentieth of her total repertoire of the finest songs of the black tradition, songs that were so profound, true and compelling that they were adopted immediately by the Georgia Sea Island Singers and sung on concert stages across the country. There are more books to be written about Bessie Smith Jones, more explorations that should be mounted into the depth and range of her experience, her art, her determination to keep the faith with those who came before her, to keep on singing the songs the way they were supposed to be sung. We have not yet begun to learn all that she had to teach nor listened to all that she had to say.

This life-loving, deep-rooted, confident, joyful, adventurous and astonishing woman sang in public for the last time in August 1984 at the Georgia Sea Island Festival on St. Simon's, an annual celebration that she had helped start and that has since been continued in her memory. She sat in a great chair on the stage throughout the long afternoon, I was told, with her island friends and their children around her, dozing off occasionally but rousing herself to listen and approve the performances. When it came her turn, she needed to be helped to the microphone, but she sang one of her favorite songs, a song that will always be identified with her, an old-time spiritual learned from her fore-parents, "So Glad I'm Here."

This book is dedicated to her memory.

Introduction

This book is really about one of the ways of growing up in the United States. In part, it is a memoir—the long rememberings of a Negro woman born in the Southern poverty belt around the turn of this century, a detailing of the mind and body and heart skills she learned in her "days coming up." As set down here, the games and dances that she remembers form a kind of double image, for throughout them moves a sense of the shape and thrust of the crowded, impoverished, life-demanding, life-loving complex of the Negro family of fifty years ago.

Mrs. Bessie Jones, one of the authors of this book, was born sixty-five years ago in Dawson, Georgia—a small black farming community—and grew up like thousands of other girls of her time in the rural South. She started to work when she was still a child, helping out her big family; she chopped cotton, planted potatoes, watched out for the littler children, took her schooling when her family could spare her and as it was offered. Her formal education ended when she was ten.

Balanced on the edge of real poverty almost all her life, she learned early how to amuse and entertain herself and others. Music—especially singing—is not only one of the least expensive art forms; it is also one in which you can participate while you are doing something else. There was a great deal of singing in Mrs. Jones's family; it didn't cost a cent or take any time away from the job to be done. Her maternal and paternal grandparents had sung while they worked in the fields during slavery times; some of the songs their little granddaughter learned from them were then well over a hundred years old. Mrs. Jones's mother was a fine singer and dancer; though her father never sang, "he could play any instrument you gave him."

Dawson itself must have been a musical community during Mrs. Jones's childhood. She speaks lovingly of the beautiful singing of the "old people" in the little community church on Sundays, of weekday mornings in the same small building, turned schoolhouse until the next Sunday, when the schoolteacher would lead the children in morning hymns and school songs. She tells of the long Southern twilights, when the grownups would be busy with their own affairs and the children would run outside to their games and mock dances.

I remember a hundred games, I suppose; I would say a hundred because there are so many of them. We had all kinds of plays; we had house plays, we had outdoor plays. Some of the plays have songs, some have just plays—you know, just acts or whatnot. . . . In my time coming up, the parents they would give quiltings and they would have songs they would sing while they were quilting and we would listen at those songs. And we would have egg crackings and taffy pullings and we would hear all those things—riddleses and stories and different things. That's why I'm so loaded. . . . And then I has a great remembrance of those things, that's another thing about it.

Bessie Jones, "loaded" as she was with games and songs and her own particular and irrepressible joy in living, got married and moved to her husband's home, St. Simons Island, one of the long string of coastal islands that edge the eastern shoreline of North America. There she met the Georgia Sea Island Singers, a Negro choral group whose early period has been described in a book by Mrs. Lydia Parrish (see Bibliography). The Singers, dedicated to the preservation of the old musical ways of their forebears, were so impressed with Mrs. Jones's buoyant personality, extensive repertoire, and experienced singing style that they invited her to join their group; she became one of the only mainlanders ever so honored. Mrs. Jones, in her turn, felt at home with the Singers' dignity and with their pride in their African and Afro-American heritage—the same kind of dignity and pride that had been so carefully taught her by her own parents and grandparents.

During the summer of 1964, Mrs. Jones and I met together in California to engage in a highly unusual educational experiment. Together with four other members of the Georgia Sea Islanders,* we presented a two-week workshop for Californians in which we attempted to teach some of the games, dances, and songs of the Negro South. The Singers—led by Mrs. Jones when we were dealing with children's activities—took on the somewhat unfamiliar formal responsibility of teachers; I functioned as organizer and interlocutor. The events of those crowded and productive weeks actually germinated this book.

We met from two to four hours every day with a shifting group of white Californians as students, perhaps twenty at a time: some teenagers, a few children, mothers, fathers, teachers, recreation specialists, dancers. Every day the same scene would be repeated. Mrs. Jones would urge everyone on their feet to play; the students, meanwhile, with pencils and notebooks ready, waited to be told *what* to play and *how* to play it. The white students, myself included, were desperately anxious to know what was going to happen, to understand the "rules"; then we could decide whether to play this particular game or not. After all, we might be asked to do something we didn't know how to do; we would perhaps be awkward, everyone would see our failure, we would "lose."

The impasse was finally resolved by having the Singers demonstrate first; they would play the game for us and we would then repeat it. The Islanders thought this was all rather silly, but for me, this arrangement provided a fascinating double perspective. As I watched first the Islanders and then the students, it seemed to me that the *game* was the same (we had learned the "rules") but the *play* was not (our emotional commitment and consequent emotional gratification was different). As the Singers, most of them grandparents, several in their sixties, danced their way through countless repetitions of "Little Johnny Brown" with fresh joy and humor each

* John Davis, Peter Davis, Emma Ramsey, and Mabel Hillary. Mr. Ed Young of Memphis, Tennessee, though not a regular member of the Singers, also joined us.

time, it seemed to me that I could never recall having played any game with that much involvement, that much gaiety, even as a child. Other white students confirmed my impression; we had all played games, but not quite that way, somehow.

Looking back on it now, the situation seems obvious: with all the mutual goodwill in the world, we did not really have the same thing in mind at all. Some of the conflicts were plain at the time; others became clearer in later reflection. To summarize them briefly, where the one group (white) anticipated competition, the other (black) expected cooperation and mutual support. Where one promoted individual skill and achievement, the other wanted general participation. Where one insisted on knowledge of and compliance with a set of rules, the other stressed dramatic interpretation and perceptiveness. Those of us who thought of games in terms of winning or losing were especially frustrated; there were no winners and few losers. I think most of the white students felt that we were not really playing games at all; we were doing something else, but what it was, we weren't sure.

A verbal cue from Mrs. Jones was, for me, the key to the problem. Folklorists have often reported the Negro use of the noun "play" where a non-Negro might say "game." This had never seemed especially significant to me; I assumed the terms were interchangeable. Then one day, referring to "Bob-a-Needle," Mrs. Jones remarked, "That's a game. Of course it's a play, too, but really it's a *game*."

Checking back through my taped interviews, I discovered that Mrs. Jones did indeed use the nouns "play," "game," and "dance" to refer to different items in her repertoire, and in a logical and definable way. She referred to abstract (nonmimetic) movement patterns, especially when performed by couples, as "dances." (Rudimentary "dances," seeming to function largely as rhythm and motion practice for the very young, she called "jumps" or "skips.") The term "game" she reserved not exactly for competitive but rather for conditional sequences of actions. For example, in "Bob-a-Needle," *if* you are caught with the needle, you pay a forfeit; *if* you pass it on successfully, you do not.

By far the bulk of her repertoire, however, she called "plays." Suddenly it occurred to me that the noun "play" has more than one meaning; in addition to being, according to Webster's, "exercise or action for amusement or diversion," it can also be "a drama . . . a composition . . . portraying life or character by means of dialogue and action."

Using this second definition as a starting point, the special quality of fun the Sea Islanders were having became clearer. When they "played," they were constructing over and over again small life dramas; they were improvising on the central issues of their deepest concerns; they were taking on new personalities for identification or caricature; they were *acting*.

Over half the repertoire of amusements contained in this book, then, are "plays" and should be regarded as such. They are ceremonials, small testimonies to the ongoingness of life, not miniature battles. In order to be enjoyed properly, therefore, they must be done properly—that is, joyfully and humorously but with an underlying seriousness of intent to make it all come out right, to make, as Mrs. Jones says so often and so touchingly, "a beautiful play."

Even the "games" have their basis in dramatic action; the difference seems to be in the possibilities for variation in the outcome of the plot. Competition is present, but it is on an extremely simple and unelaborate level. (I found, for example, no specialized and exclusive name for "it." Mrs. Jones did not use the term at all; when there was such a player, he was referred to casually as "the one in the middle" or "the counter.")

Both games and plays, however, are full of dramatic confrontations and conflict, the games perhaps more openly. The world the Southern Negro child awakes to every morning is a complex and often brutal one. The openly dramatized content of his reflections upon this world is apt, therefore, to be very down-to-earth. Both games and plays deal with realistic situations: getting food, quarreling with your mother, finding a "partner," working. And though the action is, in a dramatic sense, "realistic" and emotionally satisfying, the comment of the accompanying songs is frequently ironic and detached.

Two further factors important to both games and plays should be mentioned. Almost all must be performed by a group; thus all dramatic conflict is worked through in public, so to speak. Secondly, almost all involve both music and dance, and thus nearly the whole range of expressive behavior available to human beings is called upon.

Most of the above ideas came through to me first while I was actually playing the games. Mrs. Jones was right; there is no play until play begins. Though I had "known" for a long time that gesture and motion are forms of communication, I had never *felt* before, for example, that when you turn your back on someone you truly reject him. And when each of us stepped out into the center of the ring while the group stood and clapped for us, I think all the white students felt a sudden panic. There was no one to compete with, no one to compare ourselves to, nothing in our cultural experience had prepared us for this moment when we must say by our actions what we were, ungraded and unranked. The Islanders knew that the clapping group was signaling their support; the white students clapped and watched to see if they couldn't do it better.

However, most important in explaining the meaning of these games to me—the why as well as the how—were the sensitive and accurate comments of Mrs. Jones. Most of the real ideas, as well as the repertoire of games, in this book are hers.

All her life she has taken care of children—her little brothers and sisters, neighbor children, her own babies and grandbabies, the sons and daughters of her white employers, for whom she was both housekeeper and nurse. She speaks of the games she knows and has taught children so many times with the expertise of an educator and the joy of a participant. She declares forthrightly that her games are "good for children" and she knows just how: which help develop rhythmic coordination or big muscle skills, which promote responsiveness or sharing. She has sifted out through her memories of her own childhood the activities that meant—and still mean—most to her; she has added others to them from her more recent experience, "collecting," as do all the great folk singers, new games and plays that especially appealed to her. Today she is a carrier of the finest of that huge repertoire of children's games, family pastimes, and infant amusements of the Southern Negro family of yesterday and today.

It is important to realize, however, that when Mrs. Jones and I were talking and singing and dancing together, she was intent on transferring to me—and through me, to a wider audience—the strength and the vitality of her childhood traditions. The shadowy hurts, the fights, the fears and betrayals, the deep and hidden wounds suffered by all children, and especially by those growing up in the black South, do not appear here except by implication. She was not *documenting* anything; she was *teaching*. And as a teacher, she was passing on that part of her knowledge she considered to be "good" for children.

She may have remembered some plays which, in her mind, were of dubious value. She did not tell me these, nor did I press her for them. These are her free offerings—the best she knew—to her own people and, in a larger sense, to all children.

Santa Monica, California B.L.H.

Acknowledgments

I should first like to thank all my students who have so patiently listened while I developed and reformulated, in the guise of lectures, many of the ideas in this book.

My teaching colleagues—Edmund Carpenter, Ralph Heidsiek, Joan Rayfield, Councill Taylor, and Gregory Truex—read portions of the manuscript and were unfailingly helpful and stimulating in their comments. More distant associates—Roger Abrahams, Alan Dundes, and Brian Sutton-Smith—were kind enough to read the entire manuscript in its early stages and to cheer me on. I also owe appreciation to Mildred Johnson, Margot Slocum, Guy Carawan, Barbara LaPan, and Graham Wickham for editorial comments and assistance.

The workshop mentioned in the Introduction took place at the Idyllwild Arts Foundation, now a facility of the University of Southern California, under the direction of Max and Beatrice Krone; to them, my appreciation and thanks. Radio station KPFK and Ed Cray kindly allowed me to quote from a radio interview with Mrs. Jones.

Alan Lomax, who introduced me to Mrs. Jones, also read the manuscript, gave extensive editorial advice, and, most important, allowed me to quote from the many sensitive and skillful taped interviews he and his wife, Antoinette Marchand, had already held with Mrs. Jones.

Corey Hawes Denos, Naomi Hawes Bishop, and Nicholas Hawes typed manuscript, copied music, sang the harmony parts, tried out the directions, and took extensive field notes. I couldn't have done it without them. Baldwin Hawes not only tolerated his wife's being "with book" during an interminable period, he approved and encouraged the project in a hundred ways.

The Georgia Sea Island Singers—John Davis, Peter Davis, Mabel Hillary, Emma Ramsey, and Ed Young of Tennessee—helped both Mrs. Jones and me without stint during the entire workshop period. Their special and essential contributions are acknowledged throughout the pages that follow.

B.L.H.

Note to Parents and Teachers

Many participants in the California workshop asked me to make available or publish the games and songs they had been learning. Somehow the simple setting down of words and tunes and actions had lost its validity for me; perhaps I have absorbed too much of Mrs. Jones's point of view. The "how" had become more important than the "what" and the "why" most vital of all. So I have tried to write an instruction book which will give some clues to the understanding of all three, in the hope that parents and teachers who may use this book may come to have an appreciation for the totality of this tradition, and not just rifle it for its substance.

For this reason, I have organized the book in an unconventional way. In the first place, I have included what seemed to me relevant and useful historical data, and I have indicated where more could be found. I have also described some games as well as some adult musical activities which are obviously impractical for the average schoolyard or family; these were included for their own interest and for the insights they lend to the over-all subject. Lastly, I have grouped the games, not in over-all order of difficulty, but in the categories to which Mrs. Jones allotted them: "clapping plays," "jumps and skips," "ring plays" and so on. This will, I hope, make clear her developmental picture of how the child matures, socially and physically.

Each section is preceded by a general introduction in which the category is discussed, historical background provided, and any special techniques of dance or musicianship outlined. These section introductions also include some statements on the relative ease or difficulty of the specific games that follow. Generally, within each section, the games are arranged from "easy" to "hard."

Each game or play has its own double introduction: a brief explanatory statement attempting to set the game in historical or functional perspective;

and comments from Mrs. Jones (in italics) which pin down that quality which is so elusive, the emotional "feel" of the game.

The following statements are suggestions for teachers and parents on how to use this book. (See also directions for dance steps, pp. 44–46, and suggestions for ring play on pp. 90–91.

1. These games are an enormous amount of fun, but the real fun doesn't happen until the games are actually *played.* Leaf through the book and try different ones out, selecting, as Mrs. Jones does, those that especially appeal to you.

2. Learn the song, if it is a singing game, by singing it over and over until you have it by heart. Then change the order of the verses—or add new ones from your own imagination—as the spirit of the game *as it is being played* dictates. Once you have the pattern down, don't be afraid to change the words to fit the particular situation. One easy thing to do, for example, is to put the names of different children into such games as "Way Go, Lily."

3. The tunes of these songs are basically quite simple; some have only three or four notes. Like almost all black singers, Mrs. Jones likes to decorate her melodies with a variety of free vocal effects such as slides or scoops, some of which have been indicated by the grace notes used in the music notation. When first trying a song out, *ignore the grace notes until you have learned the basic tune* (shown in the standard sized notes). Then try adding one or two short slides up to or away from a note (as indicated by the grace notes) but do not try to emphasize them or give them a hard-and-fast fixed time value or make them into distinct, athletic vocal leaps. Their effect should be casual, like short, light *glissandi.* The great gospel singer Mahalia Jackson does a lot of this vocal ornamentation; she has been described as adding "flowers and feathers" to her songs. A "flower" or a "feather" here and there, you will find, adds greatly to the rhythmic swing and sparkle of Mrs. Jones's tunes.

4. Many of Mrs. Jones's plays are chanted rather than sung. Such chants have been written out on the music staff with "x" notes, in order to approximate the pitch pattern as well as the rhythm. When trying these, do *not* worry about absolute pitch; simply let your eye travel along the curve of the "melodic line" and follow it with your speaking voice. You will find the effect falls just halfway between speaking and singing.

5. Do *not* try to accompany the songs on the piano, or even on such portable "folk" instruments as the guitar or the auto-harp. All they need is a simple off-beat clap, as described in the introduction to "Clapping Plays." If you are playing the game yourself, as you should be, you won't have time to play an instrument anyway.

6. The singing games should be danced, not played in a "see who can get there first" spirit. The really important stylistic quality is *to move in time with the music;* the social value being expressed, I believe, is coordination of individual and group effort. This is helped enormously by the steady offbeat clapping and the rhythmic quality of the lead voice. It is much easier to sing rhythmically when you are yourself in motion; and this is why the teachers (or lead singers) should themselves be playing the game.

7. The lead singing part can be—and often is—changed "in mid-flight," while the game is going on. Children can frequently take over on the lead

once they know the song, and will do a good job of it. After all, it was their game first.

8. If there is a leading part in terms of the *action,* however, as there is in all the ring plays, be sure to give everybody a turn at it if you have to play the same game right through recess. The Islanders were always uncomfortable if we had to stop "in the middle"; it violated the basic democratic construction of the game itself.

9. Don't be afraid of what appear to be the "hard" games. A few minutes' quiet observation of children, both white and black, at work on their own tradition of singing games, jacks, jump rope, hop scotch and so on, will convince you that many adults seriously underestimate the motor capacities of children, not to mention their attention span and capacity for self-motivation.

10. Consider the possibility that some of the children, depending on their backgrounds, might already know these games or others like them. Perhaps they can teach the teacher.

11. Enjoy yourself. This is a beautiful and democratic tradition, full of joy and the juices of life. Don't be too solemn, or too organized; these are for *play.*

1:
Baby Games and Plays

If I rock this baby to sleep,
Go to sleepy, little baby,
Someday he will remember me,
Go to sleepy, little baby. . . .

Mrs. Jones and Miss Emma Ramsey and I sat one long morning around the kitchen table, drinking coffee and talking about babies.

Miss Ramsey didn't talk much. She kept saying in a mock-sad voice, "I had to go to work, when I was twelve—I never had time to learn any plays!" And then we would all laugh, because underneath the comedy was a real memory of a real little girl put to work too young, and what could you do about it now but laugh a little?

Mrs. Jones had never had much time to play with the babies herself, so the number of "infant amusements" the two ladies remembered that morning was not very large. But Mrs. Jones had thought about babies a great deal and about how to begin the long process of introducing them to the world. She had much counsel and advice for me on general matters of baby care, and as we settled down into a long, comfortable chat, she began with what was to prove her major theme: that a child's first need is to learn what it is to love and to be loved.

When you get a child or a job, [*taking care of children*] *do like I used to do—don't suffer the little childrens. Get them to sleep in a good peaceable way. Treat them like you wish to be treated.*

I think babies should be rocked at times, of course. I don't think a baby ever *should be throwed aside. It gives them—well, I don't know —I think you should rock him some anyway, if you just shake him a little while. It does something for him. He's better—like he's nursed.*

You can see sometimes when you carry him in the room and he just knows you're going to throw him away—carry him in a room and shut the door and stick a bottle or a pacifier in his mouth. And he'll just look at you, and it looks like he ain't not ready. He just know you're going to carry him in the room and throw him away, and he go to pulling to you and cleaving to you. Well, he need that cleaving to you. He need you to take a little more pains with him at that time. . . . He sure do. . . .

Like all country people, Mrs. Jones had little patience with new-fangled ways.

The poor little baby, they used to could get him to sleep. He would be normal and sleep normal, and he would have a good way of sleeping because they were normal babies. But now you don't know what he is yourself, and he don't know himself, because he drink all manners of kind of milk, you see. And the baby is supposed to be nursed off his mother's milk and none other milk but that. But now you expect him to be quiet and laugh, and he got bull's milk in him, or goat milk, or something. He can't be so quiet with all that crazy kind of milk in him. . . .

As I listened, it seemed to me that the accuracy of Mrs. Jones's information was not nearly as important as the accuracy of her feelings. In the era of the plastic shell and the infant car seat, she still thought that all babies needed to know the warmth of a human lap, the touch of human hands. At one point, she confessed with a little embarrassment,

I stretch babies too. Sometimes I get with people nowadays, their babies ain't stretched out, and I'm sitting down looking at the baby, and I slip and play with him and stretch him. . . . Their backs need to be stretched like you stretch yourself, you know? Pull his arms, you know, and his leg, and sometimes hold him in the midst of his back and have his weight pull him. That keeps his back from being humped. . . . A lot of people don't think about stretching babies; all they want to do is to lay 'em down. But he need exercise, just like your ownself. . . .

Mrs. Jones, however, does not accept tradition uncritically. She looks at procedures with the thoughtful and analytical eye of an educator; she is concerned, ultimately, with results. For this reason, though she is a tradition carrier, she does not hesitate to say when she thinks the "old peoples" were wrong.

Some things way back there I kind of disapprove with now that I've brought up children myself . . . like you telling a baby, "Tee, tee?" when you're telling him, "See, see?" I think you should tell him directly what you're saying. You should tell him, "See that?" instead of "Tee dat?" because he hear you saying that and he'll come right up saying the same thing, and you're going to have to teach him over again. I think you should speak the words pronounced right. Long years ago, when I was coming up, they didn't do it; they talked baby talk to babies, you see. But I think it's right to speak plain, or after a while you got to straighten him over again. Because a baby want to learn how to talk. . . .

She commented dryly on the not infrequent exhaustion and boredom that the most devoted of mothers sometimes feels.

I sang to babies so *much, just all church songs, you know, just sing and sing and sing, just anything I could think of. And at last one day, I jumped off on "Casey Jones." Mama come to the door, she say, "Well! I never heard nobody put no babies to sleep on 'Casey Jones'!" I had just sung on out . . . I had just sung and sung and sung, and he wouldn't go to sleep, so I got off on "Casey Jones"! I sing all manner of songs. . . . You sing some of those hymns, old draggy songs, you likely to go off to sleep with the baby. . . .*

Throughout the morning, she interlarded her advice and general comments with the little plays and songs and rhymes in the section to follow. As I thought about the whole conversation later, it seemed to me that she was showing me the starting point of all the qualities she hoped to develop in children: strong, flexible, well-coordinated bodies, rhythmic sensitivity, and most important, a quality which I find hard to name. Perhaps the best word for it is "interplay": rapport with and concern for another person, a kind of responsiveness which can sustain you even when you are alone.

Sometimes I want to break 'em out of this rocking in my lap. . . . And you ease right on the bed with 'em and continue rocking or continue patting, and you hum sometimes, just a little hum to him, and he'll hum himself—some of them will. Some babies will get that little hum to themselves. Well, he know he needs that attention, that's why. That's a great little thing to think about, he need that attention. . . . He need that humming, and that be the only way he'll get it, humming himself.

If I rock this baby to sleep,
    Go to sleepy, little baby,
Someday he will remember me,
    Go to sleepy, little baby. . . .

Go to Sleepy, Little Baby

This is a lullaby, such as getting the babies to sleep, which I love. I love so well getting the babies to sleep. . . .

This is Mrs. Jones's version of the classic Southern lullaby, sung throughout the South by white and black mothers alike. It is always sad; the poignant subcurrent of the great tragedy of slavery—the separation of mother and child—always runs through it, but Mrs. Jones's version is gentle rather than bitter.

Tune phrases (see music)

Go to sleepy, little baby, (1)
Before the booger man catch you.

All them horses in that lot, (2)
Go to sleepy, little baby.

Go to sleep, go to sleep, (3)
Go to sleepy, little baby.

Mama went away and she told me to stay (4)
And take good care of this baby.

Go to sleep, go to sleep, (3)
Go to sleepy, little baby.

All them horses in that lot, (2)
Go to sleepy, little baby.
Can't you hear them horses trot? (2)
Go to sleepy, little baby.

Go to sleep, go to sleep, (3)
Go to sleepy, little baby.

If I rock this baby to sleep, (2)
Go to sleepy, little baby,
Someday he will remember me, (2)
Go to sleepy, little baby.

Go to sleep, go to sleep, (3)
Go to sleepy, little baby.

Go to Sleepy, Little Baby

This Little Piggy

You can do that with either fingers or toes; start with the thumb. The main reason for doing that when we come up was to pop them, that's stretching the joints and giving you good joints. That'll make you have good large strong limbs. . . .

Whether played as strenuously as Mrs. Jones describes it or more easily, this familiar "infant amusement" has been a staple baby game for more than a hundred years. It is played with the baby in your lap; the parent says the following rhyme and tugs or gently pinches the toes of the baby's foot—one toe for each "pig," starting with the big one.

Emma Ramsey remembered the accompanying rhyme in the way I have most often heard it:

This little piggy went to market,
This little piggy stayed home,
This little piggy had roast beef,
This little piggy had none,
This little piggy cried, "Wee, wee, wee!" all the way home!

Mrs. Jones commented, "I heard it the way Emma said it later on up when I got to be a big girl. This was really the slavery-time way of doing it."

This little piggy wants some corn.
This little piggy says, "Where you going to get it from?"
This little piggy says, "Out of Massa's barn."
This little pig says, "Run go tell!"
This little pig says, "Twee, twee, twee, I'll
    tell old Massa, tell old Massa!"

Mrs. Jones and Miss Ramsay laughed heartily over the betrayal by the last two little pigs. I have wondered since about that laughter—and wondered, too, if the situation satirized here might not be the same one that gave rise to the "hypocrite," the "back-biter," and the "so-called friend that's easy for to bend" of the spirituals and the blues. Actually, Mrs. Jones's version is older than she realized; her poem has been recorded in books of English nursery rhymes, and may have originated among the serfs of feudal England.

Jump That Jody

I'd bounce him on my lap, and he was so heavy and my arms would get so tired. And he'd say, "Jump for Jody, Mama; jump for Jody, Mama," and he'd be so heavy and just be jumping. . . .

Mrs. Jones made up this little tune for her own first-born, but it follows a traditional pattern of baby play. Stand the baby on your lap, holding his arms stretched over his head and "jump" him up and down.

Jump that Jody, jump it,
Jump that Jody, boy.
Jump that Jody, jump it,
Jump that Jody, boy.

That's for their knees, to get their knees stretched out for walking, to get their kneecaps slipped so they won't walk funny. . . . That's why we always jumped babies; the old folks would tell us to jump them so their legs wouldn't be bowlegged.

Jump That Jody

New words and new music adaptation by Bessie Jones; collected and edited by Alan Lomax.

Ride, Charley, Ride

You mostly call your knee Charley, because it's [a horse] going to throw you. The baby sit on your knee and you're jumping it: "Ride, Charley, ride!" And sometimes a little child will get on your knee and say, "Ride, horsey!" because they know that's what you're going to do. And then you set him on astraddle if it's a boy, so he can learn to sit straddle and ride a horse that way. You set the girl on both knees or either set her sideways because you got to set her so it won't tickle and jar her stomach. You can ruin her stomach so quick inside. . . .

Throughout the Western world, "dandling" or bouncing a baby on the knee has been a favorite infant amusement. Mrs. Jones did not know the more elaborate "Ride a cock-horse to Banbury Cross" but sang her own, probably again made up for her own babies.

Ride, Charley, ride.
Ride that horsey, ride! (repeated ad lib)

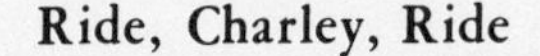

Finger Names

But in those days, they taught *you things. . . .*

Mrs. Jones is speaking here about her school years, a period which she remembers with affection and pride, even though, as she wrote me once, "I never has went to school a whole term and I didn't get past the fifth grade; every school day I had to keep other people's babies, and sometimes I had to work in the fields."

But Mrs. Jones's teacher, whom she often quotes, did indeed teach her many things, including such traditional lore as the names of the fingers. In older times each finger, like the thumb, had indeed a separate name: in England, the names are sometimes still given as thumb, toucher, longman, lecheman (for the doctor, who used that finger in tasting medicines or applying ointment), and finally, littleman.

Such names are often recited while tugging on the baby's fingers, in the same way that the toes are pulled while "This Little Piggy" is recited. Mrs. Jones, however, did not use these names for play purposes but as part of her vocabulary.

You call 'em Tom Thumb, dog finger, middle finger, no finger, and little finger. We had a teacher taught us that back in Dawson, Georgia. He give us to understand that the no finger [ring finger] *is called that because it isn't much help.*

Your dog finger, that's your bad-luck finger. That dog finger causes bad luck to people, and today I don't put that finger on a sore because it's apt to cause a scar. I put salve or anything on with the middle finger. And you don't point it at people. If an old man or old lady point their dog finger at you, you know you're going to have bad luck. They'll put mouth on you with that finger—bad mouth on you. Some of those old people, when they'd point their dog finger at you, it was there—they meant that thing.

John Davis, coming in just then, told us the finger names he had learned when he was a boy on St. Simons Island: thumb, potlicker, longman, lingman, littleman. Everybody broke up over "potlicker."

Patty Cake

I think it's better to teach babies little games, to give them some consolation to be with you. As long as you're doing that [*playing games*], *they're looking dead at you, they look straight at you. . . .*

"Patty Cake" has been giving babies and their parents "consolation" for more than two centuries at least. The baby sits on your lap "looking dead at you," and the parent holds the baby's hands, clapping them together in rhythm during the first three lines of the poem to follow. During the fourth line, the baby's palms are rotated against each other, as though there were a ball of dough between them, and on the fifth line, both the baby's arms are swung to one side in a flinging motion. Then, of course, as the baby grows older, he can mirror your movements and both of you can play it independently, still face to face.

Patty cake, patty cake, baker's man.
Put it in the oven and spike it with tea,
Save it for supper for baby and me.
Roll 'em . . . roll 'em . . . roll 'em . . . roll 'em . . .
Da-a-a-a-sh 'em in the oven!

British patty cakes are little teacakes usually containing raisins; in Georgia, however, they may be different.

That play tickles the baby. D-a-a-a-sh 'em in the oven! . . . You're making batter cakes and you have tea to drink with it, you see. Looks like they would say "beat it, beat it," but they wouldn't; it was "roll it, roll it." . . . It was patty cake, like you make up the hoecake bread, you know; you pat it out in your hands. That must be what it was. . . .

Tom, Tom, Greedy-Gut

I never believe in tickling babies, because it makes them stutter. The old peoples say it makes them stammer. You can show them how to clap hands, Greedy-Gut, and different things. . . . Learn them how to use their hands.

Though I have looked carefully, I have found no reference to this play in any other collection, except for the nursery rhyme:

To bed, to bed, says Sleepyhead.
Tarry a while, says Slow.
Put on the pot, says Greedy-Gut,
We'll sup before we go!

That rhyme, however, does not seem to have a game that goes with it. The Ewe people of Ghana, however, do a social dance that is accompanied partly by drumming and partly by a pattern of alternate hand-clapping and chest-slapping almost identical to the movements Mrs. Jones makes with this play. Perhaps "Tom Tom Greedy-Gut" is a real cultural amalgam, part West African, part old English.

"Greedy-Gut" is played to entertain a lap baby, sitting facing you, preferably one who is old enough to mirror the actions. The parent holds his own hands close to his chest, claps three times, slides the right hand back to slap the chest and follows this by slapping his chest with the left hand. These movements are expanded into the following sequence; the rhythm is indicated on the second line:

Clap	clap	clap	slap	slap;	clap	slap	slap,	clap	slap	slap
1 &	2 &	3	&	4 &	1	&	2 &	3	&	4 &

This exactly matches the spoken rhythm of the first line of the couplet that follows; the second line is spoken to a more syncopated rhythm, though the clap continues to repeat the above formula.

Tom, Tom, Greedy-Gut, Greedy-Gut, Greedy-Gut.
Eat all the meat up, meat up, meat up.

Tom, Tom, Greedy-Gut

Written and adapted by Bessie Jones; collected and edited by Alan Lomax. TRO—© copyright 1972 Ludlow Music, Inc., New York, N.Y. Used by permission.

2:
Clapping Plays

If you know how *to clap and what you're clapping* for *you can come out right with the song. . . . You're supposed to have your music come out even with your singing. . . .*

In many parts of the South, the word "music" simply means any instrumental accompaniment for a song. Mrs. Jones says "music" whenever she is talking about the hand-clapping with which she and the other Islanders accompany almost every game or play or song. And their hand-clapping *is* music—in every sense of the word; it is varied and expressive and subtle, completely different from a routine beating out of the time.

Learning "how to clap" turns out to be a developmental process as Mrs. Jones describes it. It starts with the baby games, like "Patty Cake" or "Tom, Tom, Greedy-Gut," in which the child copies the parent's movements. Next, as will be seen later in this chapter, come the clapping games played with a partner, such as "Green Sally Up"; these require increased cooperation and produce more interesting tonal effects. Finally, the almost-grown child graduates to the sophistication of the elaborate solo rhythms involved in such plays as "Hambone" or "Juba."

The plays in the following section, then, deal with "how to clap"; they are little practice pieces through which the child learns and polishes his rhythmic skills. The group clapping—the real "music" that accompanies all the singing games—is a different matter. Here, as Mrs. Jones puts it, you have to know "what you're clapping *for*." And what you're clapping *for* seems to be, at least in part, the creation of a rhythmic bond, the fusion of the group into a single internally cooperative unit.

The only time I ever saw Mrs. Jones stop a game was during a practice of "Oh Green Fields, Roxie" when a player whose turn it was to take the center of the ring simply walked in at a normal pace. "You got to *dance* it, you got to play *on time*, you got to *be* on time, you got to do it *right!*" was Mrs. Jones's agonized comment. In all the singing and rhythm plays she taught, "being on time" was essentially equivalent to "doing it right."

Mrs. Jones's advice as to *how* to be on time was eminently practical. "Move your feet!" she would say to the students, and to the other Singers as well on the rare occasions when a song or a clap pattern was not developing as it should. Magically, the rhythm would steady; the group would come together. Mrs. Jones's foot "move," then, is worth some examination.

Basically, even when she was sitting down, it was a shift of weight, requiring two counts on each side. Sitting, she would place first her right foot out a bit in front, landing flat-footed, and then step with the same foot back in place, repeating the pattern with the left foot. Standing, she would step on her right foot, bring her left foot close to her right, and "step it down" *without a weight change*, repeating the pattern to the left. Though each movement was done flat-footed, as though stamping, she normally kept her footfalls quiet, except when she wanted an extra drumming effect.

As I watched, it seemed to me that this was basically a dance movement. Though restrained, it is strong; the body swings slightly with it. The movements are on the first and third beats of the measure, at the points where the dancer would probably take his strong steps.

To clap well, then, you must start with your feet, since the claps come *after* the weight changes (or "steps") and thus occur on the normally unaccented beats of the measure (the second and the fourth). The movement Mrs. Jones calls "stepping it down" (putting the foot down without changing weight) coincides with the claps.

one	two	three	four
R step	clap	L step	clap
	L (step it down)		R (step it down)

Thus the performer finds that his feet and hands are holding a kind of conversation—feet stating, hands answering—in the classic antiphonal (or answering-back) structure that seems to underlie all American Negro music. The footfalls, however, are light; the claps are loud, so that the sounded emphasis falls on the "weak" beats, or offbeats, of the measure. Most of the time you cannot hear the "strong" beats at all, the feet step so quietly.

The basic accompaniment for all the songs in this book, with the exception of lullabies and those game-songs in which the players' hands are otherwise occupied, is the single offbeat hand-clap just described. Mrs. Jones always used it when she was singing by herself, occasionally varying it with a double offbeat clap pattern:

one	and	two	and	three	and	four	and
step		clap	clap	step		clap	clap

(Since this pattern *looks* more complicated, it may be worth pointing out that it is exactly like the single offbeat clap except that you clap twice each time instead of once.)

However, to the Sea Islanders, descendants of the great African polyrhythmic drum choirs, such patterns as the above are pretty simple stuff; they think of both the single and the double offbeat claps as only a kind of skeleton or framework for the rhythmic structures they like to build. Like Afro-American musicians throughout the country, the Sea Islanders further elaborate their rhythmic effects in two ways: varying the pitch of their percussive sounds and practicing polyrhythmic clapping (two or more rhythms being sounded out at the same time).

Pitch variation. All percussive sounds have pitch—that is, they sound "high" or "low"—but some musical systems have elaborated upon this and others have not. West Africa is one of the parts of the world where drums function almost as melodic instruments, their pitch variation is so complex. It is interesting that in West Africa, many of the native languages are "tonal"; in such languages the meaning of a word can be changed by the pitch at which it is spoken. The so-called talking drums are in part based on this quality; possibly the importance of pitch variation in the drumming style is a reflection of the importance of pitch variation in the language.

North American plantation owners during the era of slavery were well aware of the possibility that their slaves might be able to communicate from plantation to plantation by drumming and thus organize revolts. For this reason, and also because they feared that the use of drums might consolidate African religious practices and slow down the slaves' conversion to Protestantism, they made serious attempts to eliminate the playing of drums entirely. They were in part successful; the playing of real drums in the old African way almost completely died out in the United States. However, although the instruments were destroyed, the activity itself was not; Negroes did and do drum on anything available—pots and pans, the floor, their own bodies.

Body-slapping, which the old folks call "patting" and the young people call "hand jive," is especially interesting in its emphasis on pitch as well as rhythm. If you slap your thigh and then the back of your hand, you will notice that the second slap is higher in pitch than the first. Slap other parts of your body—chest, side, cheek, the top of your head—and you will discover a whole range of pitches can be sounded on your own anatomy. "Tom, Tom, Greedy-Gut" uses this principle for an infant play; a more complex development of the same idea may be seen in "Hambone" and "Juba" later in this chapter.

The Islanders carry this notion into their hand-clapping as well; they clap in three distinct pitch ranges; bass, baritone, and tenor. Anatomical structure and the hardness of the palms have something to do with each person's possible range; essentially, however, the pitch is determined by the position in which the hands are held.

To clap bass, cup your palms slightly and clap with your palms at right angles to one another; the fingers do not strike together at all, only the palms. The sound should be dull, not popping.

To clap baritone, the left palm is cupped and struck with the fingers, slightly cupped, of the right hand; again the clapping motion is crosswise, one hand at a right angle to the other. (Mrs. Jones described this position once: "Let your hand be just a little bit folded where the wind can catch them four fingers.") A strong baritone clap on a hard palm can sound like a pistol shot.

Tenor is clapped variously, depending on how high you want the sound; sometimes it is clapped like the baritone, except that the left palm and right fingers are *not* cupped. To get the highest pitch of all, strike the fingers of both hands together in a flattened-out but relaxed position.

This type of clapping is not a casual stunt. The Islanders hear these various pitches as parts of a percussion orchestra; they can be as pained by a feeble or uncertainly pitched clap as a symphonic musician would be by a badly tuned violin. Further, they feel that group clapping should be balanced; if there are too many people clapping in the baritone range, someone should change over and clap tenor or bass. But the various ranges of pitch are rarely clapped simultaneously; each part normally takes on its own rhythmic pattern, resulting in a demonstration of another essentially African musical principle: the sounding of several rhythms at the same time.

Polyrhythm. Each person in a group clapping "music"—that is, accompanying a song—may either duplicate, at his own pitch, a rhythm being taken by another person, or he may perform variations on his own; with experienced clappers, the latter is invariably the case. Essentially the Sea Islanders' clapping patterns seem to cluster around the following framework:

	one	and	two	and	three	and	four	and
Baritone			X				X	(X)
Bass	X			X			X	
Tenor		X	(X)	X	(X)	X	(X)	X

This should be thought of as the core pattern; each part may be (and is) varied extensively according to the following principles:

The baritone clap is invariably the lead clap as well as the solo clap; when in doubt, clap baritone. The baritone part is also the one most generally duplicated by other clappers; it should be the strongest and the loudest, since all the other rhythmic parts are established by the baritone beat (which is, of course, the single off-beat pattern previously discussed). The bass clap may be extended into a "shave and a hair cut; six bits" pattern and infinitely varied in other ways. However, in spite of the fact that the bass pattern generally starts on the count of "one," the baritone clap invariably precedes by a measure or two the start of the bass clap and sets the fundamental tempo. The tenor clap acts as punctuation in between the other two.

The Islanders, of course, don't count their rhythmic patterns out; they "feel" them and do them. Learners will likely have to count, but some of the "feeling" that makes this complex musical interplay possible may be made clearer by the following incident. Taping one day, I wanted to be sure I had captured each rhythmic part clearly and asked the Islanders to record for me, starting their clapping parts consecutively. I asked Mrs. Jones, who always clapped lead baritone, to begin and explained that I wanted Miss Emma Ramsey, the group's stellar tenor clapper, to come in next so, as I put it, "I can see how her clap rhythm works against yours." Mrs. Jones smiled gently. "Emma don't clap *against* me; she claps *with* me."

Suddenly the cultural gulf between us yawned very wide indeed. To me, as to all white Americans, I suspect, a person who is "with" me must do just what I am doing, must copy my movements (and my ideas and my speech and my dress and my clapping). "Clap with me, children," and all the little first-graders watch carefully to see when the teacher spanks her hands together so that they can do it then, too. To Mrs. Jones and the Sea Islanders, to be "with" somebody means to respond to them, to complement and support their silences, to fill in their statements (musical, physical, and verbal) with little showers of comment, to answer their remarks—to clap a *different* pattern.

But it is not only a different pattern, it is a sympathetic and supportive pattern, as it can be only when it is grounded in a basic shared impulse—in this situation, the foot move. This, then, is why Mrs. Jones became angry at dancers who were out of rhythm; *they* were indeed not "with" her. They had rejected the unifying principle that was holding the entire group together, and, in that rejection, they had denied the total social impulse of the music. To her they must have seemed aggressive and lonely figures. In any case, this was the only occasion on which I ever heard her imply that an individual variation was wrong.

If you know how *to clap and what you're clapping* for, *you can come out* <u>*right*</u> *with the song. . . .*

The next chapter shows the child at work, beginning to learn this complex musical tradition.

Green Sally Up

PETER DAVIS: *We always said, "Rabbit in the hatchet." When I could step it like a rabbit with a long-tailed coat and a beaver on, I could really dance it then. . . .*

As Peter Davis suggests, this rhyme could be used for dancing as well as a clapping rhythm. Mrs. Jones plays this like "Pease Porridge Hot"; children sit facing each other in pairs, alternately clapping their own and their partners' hands:

1. Each player claps his own hands. (O)
2. Players clap right hands across. (R)
3. Each player claps his own hands. (O)
4. Players clap left hands across. (L)

The above pattern may be repeated indefinitely. Significantly and characteristically, Mrs. Jones starts with step two; this brings the heavy accent (of the players' own hands being clapped together) on the offbeat, rather than on the downbeat, as white children usually play it.

R O L O R O L O
Green Sally up, Green Sally down,

R O L O R O L O
Green Sally bake her possum brown.

Asked my mama for fifteen cents
To see that elephant jump the fence.

He jumped so high, he touched the sky,
He never got back till the fourth of July.

You see that house, on that hill,
That's where me and my baby live.

Oh, the rabbit in the hash come a-stepping in the dash,
With his long-tailed coat and his beaver on.

The last couplet, "Oh, the rabbit in the hash," may be repeated over and over, either at a steady tempo or speeded up as much as three times faster. The "Green Sally" couplet functions as a refrain, and may be put in anywhere you want it.

Green Sally Up

One-ry, Two-ry

Hallibo, crackibo—that seem like driving a team. . . .

This rhyme may be clapped by two players sitting or standing face to face, alternately clapping their own and their partner's right or left hands, just as in "Green Sally Up." Or a larger group may play, standing in a circle. In this case, the children clap their neighbors' hands on either side at the same time and then their own in continuous alternation.

I have seen Los Angeles children playing this circle clap, though to different rhymes, in an even more difficult manner: clapping their neighbors' hands with right hand clapping up and left hand down; clapping their own hands together; clapping their neighbors' hands *left* hand up and *right* hand down; clapping their own hands, etc. Children can do this with enormous speed as early as the age of six. Interestingly, A. M. Jones describes just such clapping play in a child's game from West Africa.

Whether played by partners or a group, however, the clap rhythm is accented in the same manner as that of "Green Sally Up." The clap is also kept steady even through such syncopated lines as "twinkle, twankle, twenty-one."

R O L O R OL O
One - ry, two -ry, dicker-y seven,

R O L O ROL O
Halli-bo, cracki-bo, ten e-leven.

R O L O R O L O
Pee, po, must be done,

R O L O R O L O
Twin-kle, twan-kle, — twen - ty one.

Mrs. Jones adds that this rhyme and the one that follows ("One Saw, Two Saw") may be used as counting-out rhymes to determine who is to be the "it" in such games as "Bob-a-Needle" or "Hide and Seek." Further, she sometimes uses this rhyme (or "One Saw, Two Saw") in place of the rhyme said in "Engine Rubber Number Nine." (See Outdoor Games.)

One-ry, Two-ry

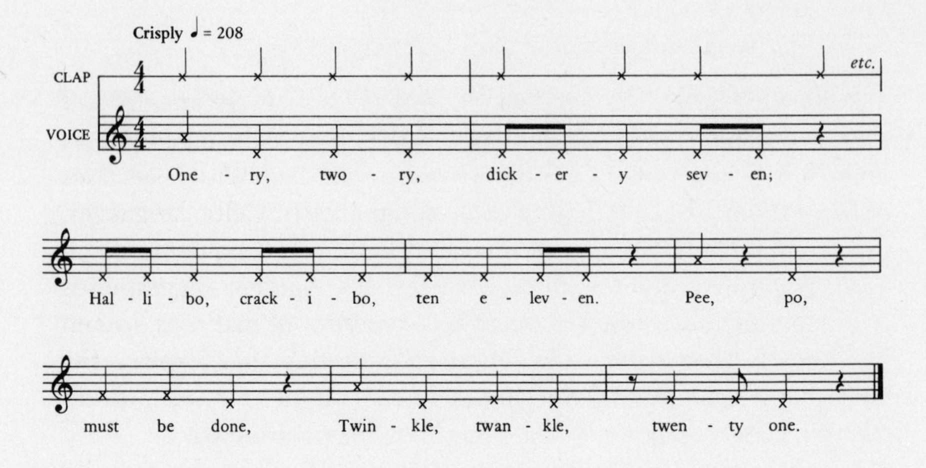
Crisply ♩ = 208
CLAP
VOICE
etc.
One - ry, two - ry, dick - er - y sev - en;
Hal - li - bo, crack - i - bo, ten e - lev - en. Pee, po,
must be done, Twin - kle, twan - kle, twen - ty one.

One Saw, Two Saw

I don't know where Mary come in at, but she's there. . . .

Both "One Saw, Two Saw" and "One-ry, Two-ry" are ancient and extraordinarily widespread rhymes. Scholars have debated over their origin for a long time. One theory traces the "nonsense" syllables of these rhymes to a method of counting in ancient Celtic languages, practiced in Great Britain since before the Roman conquest and still persisting in remote areas of the British Isles. Another suggestion is that some of the words are street-boy parodies of Latin as spoken by the educated during the Middle Ages; this may explain the presence, which troubles Mrs. Jones, of the Virgin Mary in a child's rhyme. In any case, these verbal formulas are centuries old.

For the game, the clapping pattern is started off by slapping the partner's hands first, then your own, as in "Green Sally Up" and "One-ry Two-ry."

R O L O R O L O
One saw, two saw, ziggy zaw zow,

R O L O R O L O
Bob-tail domin-icker deedle dall dow.

R O L O R O L O
Hail-em, scail-em, Vir-gin Ma-ry,

R O L O R O L O
Ike to my link-tum Buck!

One Saw, Two Saw

Head and Shoulder, Baby

The children do it pretty because they're on time; they can do that knee and ankle and be right back there on time.

With its jazzy beat, "Head and Shoulder" appears to be a fairly modern game. Although, as Mrs. Jones points out, it requires good coordination, it has turned up in city schoolyards across the country, where it appears to be mostly performed by girls. Girls seem to prefer partner-style clapping games such as this one, while their brothers are working out with solo hand jive (see "Hambone").

FORM: Though this game can be (and probably should be) practiced alone, Mrs. Jones says it should be done by partners standing and facing each other. Both chant and sing the rhyme.

VOICES	ACTION
Head and shoulder, baby,	Players touch their own heads, shoulders, and heads again.
One, ——	Players clap right hands across and then their own hands.
Two, ——	Players clap left hands across and then their own hands.
Three.	Players clap right hands across.
Head and shoulder, baby,	Players touch their own heads, shoulders, and heads again
One, ——	Players clap right hands across and then their own hands.
Two, ——	Players clap left hands across and then their own hands.
Three.	Players clap right hands across.
Head and shoulder,	Players touch their own heads and shoulders.
Head and shoulder,	Repeat.
Head and shoulder, baby,	Players touch heads, shoulders, heads.
One, ——	Players clap left hands across and then their own hands.
Two, ——	Players clap right hands across and then their own hands.
Three.	Players clap right hands across.
Knee and ankle, baby, One, two, three.	As above except players touch their own knees, ankles, and knees again.

Knee and ankle, baby,
One, two, three.
Knee and ankle, knee and ankle,
Knee and ankle, baby,
One, two, three.

Milk the cow, baby, One, two, three. Milk the cow, baby, One, two, three. Milk the cow, milk the cow, Milk the cow, baby, One, two, three.	As above except the players act out milking a cow, first with right hand, then left, and then right again.
Throw the ball, baby, One, two, three. Throw the ball, baby, One, two, three. Throw the ball, throw the ball, Throw the ball, baby, One, two, three.	As above except players act out throwing a ball.
I ain't been to Frisco, And I ain't been to school; I ain't been to college But I ain't no fool.	No action; Mrs. Jones occasionally "acted it out."
To the front,	Players jump toward each other (both feet).
To the back,	Players jump back from each other (both feet).
To the front,	Players jump toward each other.
To the back,	Players jump away from each other.
To the si- si- side,	Players jump (both feet) right, left, and right.
To the si- si- side!	Repeat; left, right, and left.

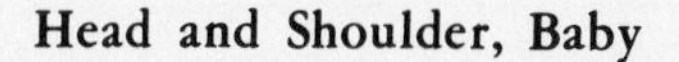

Words and music by Bessie Jones; collected and edited with new material by Alan Lomax.

Hambone

You just say it, and then you say it with your hands.

"Hambone" probably refers to the part of the anatomy most involved in playing this hand jive game, though there is undoubtedly more to it than that. Most young black men, I find, know it in one version or another.

"Hambone" may be performed alone or with a group all jiving together. While the rhyme is being said, the players slap their thighs lightly on the offbeat. *After* each line of the poem, they "pat" in the following rhythm:

(The foregoing pattern is not exactly what you expect to hear; it is, however, what Mrs. Jones does.)

The "patting" may be done on one side of the body only, using the right hand and thigh; or on both sides at the same time in parallel motion. The triplet phrase is done as follows:

1. Slap the side of the thigh with the palm of the hand in an upward brushing motion.
2. Continuing the upward brushing; strike the side or the chest with the palm of the hand.
3. Strike the thigh downward with the back of the hand.

Do this series twice, then slap your thigh three times. The entire pattern is repeated after each line of the following rhyme, in which Mrs. Jones starts with the "Hambone" poem until she suddenly merges into a series of verses from the familiar "Frog Went A-Courting."

VOICE	ACTION
Hambone, Hambone, pat him on the shoulder, If you get a pretty girl, I'll show you how to hold her. Hambone, Hambone, where have you been? All 'round the world and back again.	Pat thigh on the offbeat while the rhyme is being recited. (The first two lines have been underscored on the offbeat as an example.) At the end of each line of the rhyme, do the hambone "pat" as previously described.

Hambone, Hambone, what did
 you do?
I got a train and I fairly flew.
Hambone, Hambone, where did
 you go?
I hopped up to Miss Lucy's door.
I asked Miss Lucy would she
 marry me.
(in falsetto) "Well, I don't care if
 Papa don't care!"
First come in was Mister Snake,
He crawled all over that wedding
 cake.
Next walked in was Mister Tick,
He ate so much that it made him
 sick.
Next walked in was Mister Coon,
We asked him to sing us a wed-
 ding tune.
Now Ham- . . .
Now Ham- . . .

On one occasion, Mrs. Jones improvised a way of playing "Hambone" in which she tapped an answering rhythm with her feet instead of "patting."

heel toe heel toe
L R L R L R L R

The group followed her pattern, and soon things were going so well that she superimposed the following clap:

"Oh, he's *hamming* it!" she said, in great satisfaction.

Hambone

♩ = 208
PATTING
VOICE
Ham - bone, Ham - bone, pat him on the shoul - der,
If you get a pret - ty girl, I'll show you how to hold her.
Ham - bone, Ham - bone, where have you been?
All 'round the world and
back a - gain.
etc.

Juba

That's one of the oldest plays I think I can remember our grandfather telling us about, because he was brought up in Virginia. He used to tell us about how they used to eat ends of food; that's what "juba" means. They said "jibba" when they meant "giblets"; we know that's ends of food. They had to eat leftovers.

He used to say they would take mixed-up food and put it together, that they had to eat out of those long troughs—mush, and cush, and all that stuff put together and put plenty milk in it. But he live a hundred and five years, so, I can't say that made him live but I say it didn't kill him. And I'm up here a long time too; I never eat like that, but yet and still he have taught us a many a time how he did that. . . .

Mrs. Jones is right; this is one of her oldest rhymes. George Washington Cable saw African slaves doing a dance called "the Juba" in New Orleans' Congo Square long before emancipation; today it may be seen in some of the Caribbean Islands. In the United States, occasional mention of "juba" may be found in songs, generally associated with hand-clapping, but the dance itself appears to have been lost.

The word "juba" is probably a variation of one of the West African day names, which were often used also for girls' given names. In the United States, the original African meaning has long since been forgotten; and, as Mrs. Jones ingeniously suggests, the word may have become associated with the like-sounding English word "giblets." Here is the Juba rhyme, with Mrs. Jones's explanation of each line given in parentheses:

<table>
<tr><td>Juba this and Juba that</td><td>(That means a little of this and a little of that.)</td></tr>
<tr><td>And Juba killed a yellow cat</td><td>(That means mixed-up food might kill the white folks. And they didn't care if it did, I don't suppose.)</td></tr>
<tr><td>And get over double trouble, Juba.</td><td>(Someday they meant they would get over double trouble . . .)</td></tr>
<tr><td>You sift-a the meal, you give me the husk,
You cook-a the bread, you give me the crust.</td><td>(You see, so that's what it mean—the mother would always be talking to them about she wished she could give them</td></tr>
</table>

You fry the meat, you give me the skin,
And that's where my mama's trouble begin.
And then you Juba,
You just Juba.

some of that good hot cornbread or hot pies or hot whatnot. But she couldn't. She had to wait and give that old stuff that was left over. And then they began to sing it and play it. . . .)

Juba up, Juba down,
Juba all around the town.
Juba for ma, Juba for pa,
Juba for your brother-in-law.

(That mean everywhere,)
(All around the whole country.)

(See, that meant everybody had juba. And they made a play out of it. So that's where this song come from; they would get all this kind of thing off their brains and minds. . . .)

"Juba" may be played alone. If there is a group present, normally one person acts as lead singer-clapper while the rest dance. During section A, all do the Juba "pat" (see page 22). During sections B and C, the lead singer may clap for the rest, who dance, either individually or in couples.

LEAD VOICE	ACTION
A. Juba, Juba	All pat thighs alternately.
Juba this and Juba that And Juba killed a yellow cat And get over double trouble, Juba. You sift-a the meal, You give me the husk; You cook-a the bread, You give me the crust, You fry the meat, You give me the skin, And that is where my mama's trouble begin. And then you Juba, You just Juba.	All do Juba pat, which continues to the end of this section.
B. (Lead singer starts single off-beat clap.) Say, Juba up, Juba down, Juba all around the town. Juba for ma, Juba for pa,	Dancers "jump for joy" alone or with partner. (See p. 44.)

Juba for your brother-in-law.
You just Juba, Juba.

C. (Lead singer starts double off-beat clap)
Let's Juba this and Juba that,
And Juba killed a yellow cat;
You get over double trouble, Juba.
You sift-a the meal, you give me the husk
You cook-a the bread, you give me the crust,
You fry the meat, you give me the skin,
And that's where my mama's trouble begin,
And that's where my mama's trouble begin.

Dancers continue jumping for joy.

Juba pat: (L) Slap left thigh with left hand.
(LB) Slap back of left hand with right hand (left hand should be raised from thigh).
(L) Slap left thigh with left hand.
Repeat on other side:
(R) Slap right thigh with right hand.
(RB) Slap back of right hand (raised) with left hand.
(R) Slap right thigh with right hand.

Continue, alternating from one side to the other. This pat, when speeded up, has a kind of galloping triple-time "Hi-yo Silver" effect. Since this essentially triple rhythm is carried evenly over a four-beat rhyme, the effect is extremely syncopated.

L	LB	L	R	RB	R	L	LB	L	R	RB	R	L	LB	L
Ju	ba	this	and	Ju	ba	that	and	Ju	ba	killed	a	yel	low	cat

R	RB	R	L	LB	L	R	RB	R	L	LB	L	R	RB	R	etc.
And	get	o	ver	doub		le	troub	le	Ju	ba					

They be dancing, then, you see; the children be jumping—we call it dancing, which it is. They be jumping. Nowadays I have the children do the Charleston with it, have the boys do their knees together like they cutting scissors. I learned the Charleston, way back in Miami time—nineteen and twenty-five. . . . I didn't never do it, but I prayed for the rest of them that did.

Juba

♩ = 168-176
PATTING
VOICE
(see directions) etc.
Ju - ba, Ju - ba, Ju - ba this and Ju - ba that and
Ju - ba killed a yel - low cat and get o - ver doub - le troub - le, Ju - ba. You
sift - a the meal,_ you give me the husk;_ You cook - a the bread,_ you
give me the crust._ You fry the meat,_ you give me the skin,_ And
that is where my ma - ma's troub - le be - gin._ And then you Ju - ba, You just
CLAP
etc.
Ju - ba. Say Ju - ba up,_ Ju - ba down,_ Ju - ba all_ a - round the town.
Ju - ba for ma,_ Ju - ba for pa,_ Ju - ba for your bro - ther - in - law. You just Ju - ba,
CLAP
etc.
Ju - ba. Let's Ju - ba this and Ju - ba that, and Ju - ba killed a yel - low cat; You
get o - ver doub - le troub - le, Ju - ba. You sifta the meal, you give me the husk, You
cooka the bread, you give me the crust, You fry the meat, you give me the skin, And
that's where my ma - ma's troub - ble be - gin, And that's where my ma - ma's troub - le be - gin.

3:
Jumps and Skips

And use your feet. You hardly can clap without using your feet, not and stay on time. . . . That [clap] didn't go so good for me, because you've got to get it all over, and use your feet, see? . . .

The more I watched Mrs. Jones and the Islanders, the more convinced I became that *all* their music-making activities involved basic body movement, or what the white community would call "dance." The point is, as Mrs. Jones puts it, "you've got to get it all over." *All* singing was accompanied by swaying, weight shifts, and hand, head, and body movements of greater or less degree, all suggesting a dance that was not yet quite visible. Their "real" dances seemed, then, simply broader, more explicit statements of the dances they were already doing while they "stood still" to sing.

The Islanders' point of view toward their dance style, however, was considerably more sophisticated than mine. Dancing, to them, was a highly elaborated activity, organized into long series of "steps," each with its own descriptive name. This tradition is an old one; in the minstrel theater the white vaudevillians in blackface (who had learned their trade through careful observation of Negro dancers) were experts in the Pigeon Wing, the Double Shuffle, and the Turkey Trot as early as the 1840's.

I myself was able to learn only a few of the Islanders' steps—

those Mrs. Jones considered suitable for children's dance (and a few others that slipped by her). Most were dramatic or imitative in nature but highly formalized. Here it might be useful to point out that American Negroes, contrary to popular legend, are not "free" in their dancing. They do not fling themselves about; their bodies are under strict control at all times, like those of all good dancers.

The "rules" I was able to absorb are few but important. The foot keeps contact with the ground as much as possible, and full contact at that. All dancing is done flat-footed; this is extremely difficult for Euro-Americans, whose first approach to a dancing situation is to go up on their toes. (A clear mental picture of the difference in basic foot position might be gained if Bill Robinson's and Fred Astaire's tap dancing styles could be visualized.)

The foot is generally set down flat—all at once—neither toe-heel nor heel-toe; and foot swings, jumps, and kicks are kept "low and draggy." Most up-and-down motion is gotten by bending and straightening the knees. If you try walking with knee and foot action as described, you will find that the hips are forced out behind slightly and that the trunk movement will be a slight swing forward and back, *not* side to side. The Islanders regarded exaggerated hip swings or hip rotation as vulgar.

The upper part of the body is erect but supple; the body often bows forward slightly. The arms are loose but not flapping, the shoulders often revolving slightly. In many dances, the shoulder movement alternates, first right, then left; in the "buzzard lope" step, the shoulders move together like wings.

Overall, all movements are loose and supple; most whites dance far too tensely. All movement is restrained as well; though the sex of the dancers is obvious, the dancing is not elaborately "sexy."

The following is a cataloguing of the steps called for in this book, only a fraction of the Islanders' total repertoire.

JUMP FOR JOY. A strongly restrained Charleston step, with the high side kick eliminated; the feet should be kept as close to the ground as possible.

BALL THE JACK. Holding the legs together from foot to hip, rotate the knees in a circle; this obviously rotates the hips also. Mrs. Jones seemed to feel this was mildly improper for small children—the sort of thing that you should tell them not to do, but you know they are going to do it anyway.

SNAKE HIPS. This, on the other hand, is a little bit scandalous, whether performed by child or adult. The movement is the same, but the knees are not kept together and move forward and back, first one knee, then the other. Mrs. Jones made a strong distinction between balling the jack and doing snake hips, both in the techniques—which she had verbalized—and in their social propriety.

STEP IT DOWN. This term refers both to the side-to-side movement that Mrs. Jones always makes when she sings and claps, as described in the introduction to Chapter 2 (p. 20), *and* to a formal dance step. The *dancer* "steps it down" in a forward-and-back motion: one—put the foot out in front as though stepping on something but do not change weight; two—put the same foot back in place and step on it, changing weight; repeat with the other foot to a count of two on each side. Thus the dancer, in contrast to the clapper, syncopates by weight changes on the *second* and *fourth* beats.

ZUDIE-O. This is simply a two-step: step, slide, step, to a count of one and two (rest), as in the fox trot. (See the dance by the same name for a fuller description.)

RANKY TANK. Dance teachers would refer to this as a "buzz step"; the actual motion is rather like riding a scooter. The weight is on the forward foot, and the back foot pushes the dancer along the floor in a short shoving motion to a count of one, two.

BUZZARD LOPE. The Islanders knew a complex religious dance by this name, a description of which is beyond the scope of this book. They also use the term, however, to indicate a movement that appears in children's (or nonreligious) dance. In this latter context, the term means to turn the body at the waist so that one shoulder is pointing forward, and revolve both shoulders in parallel motion, forward to back. The arms are held loosely bent at the elbows, and the shoulder movement then makes the elbows stand out and flap slightly, like wings.

SHOUT. This term is also used in two different contexts: religious and secular, in neither of which does it mean anything to do with the voice. The word itself comes from an Arabic term "saut," meaning, loosely, to dance. The nonreligious shout step appears in several traditional children's plays as follows: with weight on the active foot, give a little shove backward as though hopping without the foot leaving the floor; dancers sometimes call this movement a "chug." While "chugging" back on the right foot, swing the left foot forward. Step on the left foot and "chug" it backward while swinging the right foot forward. This is done to a count of two: step, chug. The ultimate result, by the way, is that you stay in the same place.

SANDY REE. An extension of the shout step to a count of four: step, step, step, chug. The positioning of the feet is also more elaborate; for a full description, see the dance by the same name.

POSSUM-LA. A shuffling jump, landing on both feet, almost like a two-footed "chug." The dancer lands heavily, at the same instant bending both knees sharply.

MAKE A MOTION. This is the moment of improvisation. Faint hearts simply perform a standard step they know; more experienced dancers make their own statement, depending on the way they are feeling at the moment. Since the call to "make a motion" (sometimes, "make *your* motion") often occurs in courtship plays, the opportunity for personal display of agility, coordination, and finesse of movement brings out the best in the dancers.

Some further discussion on the question of percussive dancing may be useful. On the whole, the Islanders all danced in a relatively soft-footed manner, with only occasional stomps and heel knocks. When these occurred, they seemed to serve the function of rhythmic accenting rather than to be actual parts of the dance *movement*. My whole impression was that their floor sounding—any kind of tapping or stamping—was actually a kind of *musical* accompaniment, was, indeed, a substitute for an absent drum.

Mrs. Jones definitely used her feet as instruments to accompany her singing. Her strong, simple foot movement when she sang standing up has already been described. When she was relaxed and sitting back in a chair, her foot-tapping became considerably more complex.

Her usual rhythm was a rapid soft sounded double beat performed in one of two ways: tapping with the toe of one foot and the heel of the other simultaneously, and then reversing; or a steady double-timed soft stamp with the left foot, while the right foot tapped alternately with the heel and the toe. As we practiced this, she would laugh at me if I could not sound both my feet at *exactly* the same instant. Then, anxious like all great teachers to turn a failure into a positive experience, she would announce proudly that I had made "a double beat!"

This rapid, soft, steady tapping (normally eight counts to every four-four measure) could be varied at will by occasional rhythmic breaks, which she usually put in at the end of the poetic line of the song or during rests in the melody. Again, I felt that at these moments, the tapping feet were playing a responsive "tune" back to the voice, just as the blues picker's guitar answers the singer between vocal phrases. Further, in these breaks each foot took on its own role, and each responded to the other: the left foot (L) kept the basic rhythm, landing flat-footed and always on the counts of one and three, while the right foot handled the accents, sometimes flat-footed (R) and sometimes toe-heel (t-h) or heel-toe (h-t). Here are a few of the rhythms she showed me:

four and one two three; four and one two three
t h L R L t h L R L

four and one and two three; four and one and two three
t h L t h L t h L t h L

The two above combined, with the toe-heel sequence reversed:

four and one two three; four and one and two three
h t L R L h t L h t L

Another variation, with the heel leading:

four and one two and three and four; one and two three
h t L h t L h t L h t L

Her movements were small and discreet always; one could barely see her knees moving up and down under her dress skirts. The heel-toe movement was accompanied by a slight brushing forward of the foot; for the toe-heel, the foot brushed backward. Like any expert musician, she had no need to show off; she was too busy creating *music* with crisp even taps like an expert drummer's. Once she told me that she was making a "joyful noise."

In this context, one is tempted to see in the modern tap dancer a lonely figure, recreating for his own ears all the joyful noises that should be being sounded for him by hands, feet, sticks, and drum heads. And again one is puzzled by how hard it is to distinguish between *musical* values and *dance* values. Perhaps the only practical solution is the one suggested in Mrs. Jones's frequent remark, "You've got to get it *all over.*"

In the task of learning *how* to "get it all over" the jumps and skips in this chapter are again practice pieces, preparing the small child for the complications of later group play and dance. As Mrs. Jones used them, they seem to have been designed both to teach individual steps and to develop specific physical skills. Indeed, all the plays she included in this category, with the single exception of "Just from the Kitchen," can be done by a single dancer, though they are more pleasantly played by more.

Skip to the Barbershop

In a way, besides learning [at school] they got to get their exercise, too. This [play] is to keep their legs and all in good shape. . . .

Mrs. Jones speaks very affectionately about her few years of formal education in Dawson, Georgia, around the turn of the century, where school met in a one-room church house and the children spent Friday afternoons cleaning the building so that it would be ready for meeting on Sunday. Many of her plays and games she learned in school, and many of them she feels are truly educational in nature, preparing a child for later, more complex activity.

"Skip to the Barbershop" she classifies as

just a little skip, where you learn the children how to skip, because some children cannot skip. You get them in line and you can have something for them to pick up—go over to the other side of the room and pick it up and bring it back—and you tell them, "Skip to the barbershop." You can do it with untied feets or tied feets; untied feets are better. That way you see which one of the children can skip over and bring something back the fastest and the prettiest. . . .

Skip, skip, to the barbershop,
I left my hat at the barbershop
And three sticks of candy.
One for you, one for me,
And one for sister Sally.

Skip, skip, to the barbershop,
I left my coat at the barbershop, etc.

The play can continue with various other articles of clothing substituted in the rhyme for "hat" and "coat" until all the players have a turn. Though the rhyme could be recited by all the players together, Mrs. Jones usually chanted it alone, accompanying herself with a single offbeat clap.

Skip to the Barbershop

Just from the Kitchen

This is just a little skip. We'd do it in the yard or either in the house if it was raining. But it means this, you know, that the children would sometimes go to the kitchen and they'd give us some biscuits. At that time, some of the children they didn't have biscuits often. And when they'd get the biscuits, it was really fun. I think "shoo lie loo" means something like "I'm really glad!"

Though John Davis maintained that any play taking place in a circle is a "ring play," Mrs. Jones insisted on calling "Just from the Kitchen" a "skip," I suspect because it requires no center player. In this play, the lead singer, standing as part of the circle of players, calls out the "real" name of a different child in each verse; and the child whose name is sung then skips across the ring with his arms outstretched—"flying away over yonder."

Other kinds of food may be sung about, too; Mrs. Jones gave some of us handfuls of tomatoes, rabbit, meat skins, potatoes, and chitterlings as her imagination dictated. On one occasion she described this as an "after-slavery play":

He's so glad—he's free and got his own bread so he fly away over yonder. . . . He's so glad he got freedom food! . . .

FORM: Circle of children standing and clapping.

LEAD VOICE	GROUP VOICE	ACTION
Just from the kitchen,		All stand and clap.
	Shoo lie loo,	
With a handful of biscuits,		
	Shoo lie loo,	
Oh (Miss <u>Mary</u>),		Child whose name is sung
	Shoo lie loo,	skips across ring with
Fly <u>away</u> over yonder		arms outstretched, flying. (Don't flap; sail.) At other side, turn (on word "away") and clap with the others.

Just from the Kitchen

Shoo, Turkey

Well, that's a little jump. You squats and you jumps, you know, like that . . . and you do your hands this way, shooing the turkey each side. Oh, it's pretty. . . .

This "pretty little jump" begins with a stylized conversation between the leader and the group of children who stand in a line facing her. At the end of the conversation, the children turn and snake-dance through the yard, shooing the turkeys by waving their hands first to one side and then the other. The leader may dance with them but had probably better save her breath for the singing, as the dancers will get winded soon.

FORM: Line of children facing the leader.

LEAD VOICE	GROUP VOICE	ACTION
Little girl, little boy?		None.
	Yes, ma'am.	
Well, did you go downtown?		
	Yes, ma'am.	
Well, did you get any eggs?		
	Yes, ma'am.	
Well, did you bring them home?		
	Yes, ma'am.	
Well, did you cook any bread?		
	Yes, ma'am.	
Well, did you save me mine?		
	Yes, ma'am.	
(Begin offbeat clap)		
Well, shoo, shoo, shoo, turkey, Throw your feather way yonder. Shoo, shoo, shoo, turkey, Throw your feather way yonder. (Repeat above verse ad lib) I'm going to buy me another turkey,		Each child makes a quarter turn to his right and follows the end player, who leads out on a winding course. The step used is a chug in a squatting position; the arms are thrown out to right and left alternatively on each chug keeping time to the downbeats of the song.

Throw your feather way
yonder.
I'm going to buy me another
turkey,
Throw your feather way
yonder.

(Repeat ad lib)

Shoo, Turkey

Knock Jim Crow

When I was a little girl, I thought Jim Crow might have been a bird, because it was "going down to the new ground," and they always shoot them birds out of the corn. "New ground" is ground where the trees have been cut off, but it's never been planted in. So that was what I understood at the time, that was my idea. But we don't know what the old folks meant, we sure don't.

JOHN DAVIS: *I don't believe the old folks knew what they were talking about their ownselves. Anyway, they didn't tell nobody. . . .*

Probably, to begin with, "Jim Crow" was a bird, as Mrs. Jones and Mr. Davis suggest, but during the late 1820's the name became attached to a young white actor, Thomas D. Rice, who had invented a stage characterization of the "jolly, carefree" plantation slave. In this role, which rapidly became a popular stereotype in the minstrel theater, the young vaudevillian, wearing blackface and in comical rags, did a little eccentric dance while singing:

I kneel to the buzzard,
I bow to the crow,
And eb'ry time I w'eel about
I jump jis' so.

W'eel about an' turn about an' do jis' so,
An' eb'ry time I w'eel about I jump Jim Crow.

Reportedly, he had heard this refrain from an old Negro man some years earlier.

"Jim Crow" thus developed from a dance imitating the motions of birds and hunters, and quite possibly magical in nature, into a commercial caricature. No wonder the term, when used in a political context, has a bitter taste today. The Islanders, however, clearly regard this as a pleasurable dance, probably about birds, and "knock Jim Crow" with enthusiasm and alacrity.

FORM: Indefinite; group of children standing in a line or ring. There may be a lead singer, or the children may all sing together.

LEAD AND GROUP VOICE	ACTION
Where you going, buzzard? Where you going, crow? I'm going down to new ground	Step on right foot, raise left leg with knee straight (like a high goose step) and clap hands together

To knock Jim Crow.	around it; repeat, raising alternate legs until,
Up to my kneecap,	On "to" raise right knee (bent) and slap it with right hand.
	On "cap" raise left knee (bent) and slap it with left hand.
Down to my toe,___	On "to" point down to ground with right index finger.
	On beat after "toe" point down to ground with left index finger.
And every time I jump up, I knock Jim Crow. (Speed increases)	Resume raising alternate legs and clapping around them as in first step.
I knock, I knock Jim Crow. I knock, I knock Jim Crow. I knock, I knock, I knock Jim Crow. (repeat ad lib)	Dancers increase speed, continuing to lift legs and clap while turning round in place until exhaustion sets in.

Be sure that the steps are on the downbeat, so that the claps can come on the offbeat.

where	you	go	-	ing	buz	-	zard,	where	you	go	-	ing	crow?	
step		clap			step		clap	step		clap			step	clap

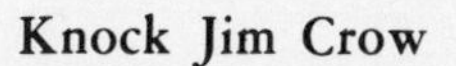

Knock Jim Crow

Josephine

This is a little play that the children all stand in a line [for]. And you stand facing them and when you call on one, it mean all, because they're all called on one name: Josephine. . . .

Like "Shoo, Turkey," "Josephine" begins with a formal conversation. This kind of prelude seems to be still another way of teaching the child responsiveness and giving him a preliminary taste of the pleasures of antiphonal singing.

At the end of the conversation, the leader sings and claps for the children, who "act out" the words with their hands while they dance the shout step (see page 45). As Mrs. Jones warns,

This is a jump . . . you got to do *it* to *do it! But the children get tired, because it's a long shout. . . .*

FORM: Line of children standing facing the lead singer.

LEAD VOICE	GROUP VOICE	ACTION
(speaking)	(speaking)	None
Josephine?		
	Ma'am?	
You want to shout?		
	Yes, ma'am!	
When?		
	Right now!	
(Chanting and clapping)		
Shout, Josephine!		Line of dancers start shout step which continues throughout without stopping until the last verse.
	Shout, shout!	
Shout, Josephine!		
	Shout, shout!	
I've got a ball of cord,		
	Shout, shout!	
I've got a ball of cord,		Dancers place one hand at back of head, feeling an imaginary knot of hair.
	Shout, shout!	
I've got a pain in my head,		
	Shout, shout!	
I've got a pain in my head,		
	Shout, shout!	Dancers put one hand to forehead.

LEAD VOICE	GROUP VOICE	ACTION
(Chanting and clapping)		
I've got a finger ring,		Dancers put index finger of one hand on other index finger.
	Shout, shout!	
I've got a finger ring.		

Shout, shout!

I've got a pain in my back,

Shout, shout!

I've got a pain in my back,

Shout, shout!

Dancers put one hand to small of back.

I've got slipper shoes,

Shout, shout!

I've got slipper shoes,

Shout, shout!

Dancers point index fingers down toward their feet.

I've got a pain in my knee,

Shout, shout!

Dancers touch knee.

I've got a pain in my knee,

Shout, shout!

I'll shake the baby,

Shout, shout!

I'll shake the baby,

Shout, shout!

Dancers hold arms as though cradling a baby, swing them from side to side.

(Singing and clapping)
Aunt Jenny's cornbread is sweet, sweet, sweet,
Take some and leave some, sweet, sweet, sweet,
Aunt Jenny's cornbread is sweet, sweet, sweet,
Take some and leave some sweet, sweet,
Take some and leave some sweet, sweet!

Dancers stop the shout step and all "jump for joy" (see page 44) until the end.

Josephine

Jazzily ♩ = 200
etc.
CLAP
VOICE
Shout, Jo - se - phine! Shout, shout! Shout,— Jo - se - phine!
Shout, shout! I've got a ball of cord, Shout, shout! I've got a ball of cord,
a fin - ger ring, a fin - ger ring,
slip - per shoes, slip - per shoes,
Shout, shout! I've got a pain in my head, Shout, shout! I've got a
pain in my back,
pain in my knee,
pain in my head, Shout, shout! I'll— shake the ba - by, Shout, shout! I'll—
pain in my back,
pain in my knee,
— shake the ba - by, Shout, shout! Aunt Jen - nie's corn - bread is
sweet, sweet, sweet, Take— some and leave some, sweet, sweet, sweet, Aunt—
— Jen - nie's corn - bread is sweet, sweet, sweet, Take— some and leave some,
sweet, sweet, Take— some and leave some, sweet, sweet.

Elephant Fair

This is just a jump; it's a play that we always played. Mama used to play it too. I have it now for the children; they stands in a line or either in a ring as they want to but they all jump, you know, dance this. It's a hard jump; it's good for you, makes you strong. I played it with the children this morning and one boy said, "Oh, tell me when to stop! Just stop me!" He was really doing it. . . .

When Mrs. Jones claps and chants this verse, accenting it strongly and expressively, the rhythm does start carrying you along and it's hard to know how to stop. The step is the "jump for joy" (described on page 44), done all the way through and speeded up on the last line for as many repetitions as your breath will allow you.

The first two lines of the verse are known all over the South; the rest is a combination of many traditional rhymes and songs. The content is rough and emotionally very satisfying, I suspect. Mrs. Jones started to laugh one day after she said the line, "Now you Alabama sucker, take your hand off of me," and remarked, "You know, we couldn't *use* words like that. We *liked* it!"

FORM: Line, circle, or other formation, if any at all. Lead singer and clapper is essential, as the dancers will be too out of breath shortly to be audible.

LEAD VOICE (chanting and clapping)	ACTION
I went down to the elephant fair,	Jump for joy.
And the birds and bees was there.	
And they went all around by the Maypole stand	
And drug their snout on the ground.	
It's the best old lady, it's the best old man;	
I like the pretty boy who totes the money.	
Old lady, old man; it's no wonder you can't stand.	
Now you Alabama sucker, take your hand off of me,	
Take your hand off of me.	
You better not mess with Lula;	
I'll tell you the reason why.	
She'll cut out your heart with a razor,	
And she'll cut out your insides too,	
And she'll cut out your insides too.	
She'll cut out your insides too (repeated ad lib)	Jump for joy speeded up faster and faster.

Elephant Fair

Pizza, Pizza, Mighty Moe

It really is pretty the way they carry it. . . . And they know it they own self, they like it, it's modern. And when they get on that thing, it's good! . . .

This fragmentary but gay curiosity is included for its own sake, as well as for what it can indicate about the current development of play. Since "Pizza, Pizza, Mighty Moe" is not an old play, the Islanders did not know how to do it, and therefore I have not seen their version performed. They did describe it, however, with considerable amusement and gusto.

Apparently they themselves saw "Pizza" at what must have been a remarkable play presented by the children of the Brunswick, Georgia, elementary school a few years ago. Both Evalina and Pizza were characters in this drama, and in one scene a chorus came out, dancing in line, one behind the other, to act out this rhyme. A generation maturing during the age of the Jerk and the Monkey would not need much instruction in how to dance to this chant; apparently, "Pizza" has caught on among the Island children as well as in Los Angeles, and, as Mrs. Jones says, "When they get on that thing, it's *good!*"

Evalina?
    Pizza, Pizza, Mighty Moe.
Well, have you seen her?
    Pizza, Pizza, Mighty Moe.
She's got a wooden leg.
    Pizza, Pizza, Mighty Moe.
But can she use it?
    Pizza, Pizza, Mighty Moe.
Oh yes, she use it.
    Pizza, Pizza, Mighty Moe.
Well, do she 'buse it?
    Pizza, Pizza, Mighty Moe.
I *know* she use it.
    Pizza, Pizza, Mighty Moe.
Well, can she ball it?
    Pizza, Pizza, Mighty Moe.
I say, *ball* it!
    Pizza, Pizza, Mighty Moe.

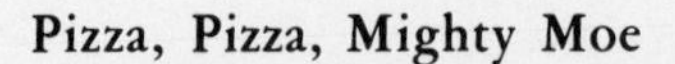

Pizza, Pizza, Mighty Moe

4:
Singing Plays

As Mrs. Jones says over and over in many different ways, children not only have to learn *how* to do something, they must also learn what they are doing it *for*. To her, the plays that teach individual skills—the claps, the jumps, and the skips—are only preparations for the moment when those developing skills are put to use within a larger context, within the group. Down from the mother's lap, away from the close one-to-one contact of the clapping plays, the growing child wanders into the larger complex whirl of the family, the play group, and the community.

The Afro-American child, both during the era of slavery and after, faced an especially difficult problem: the comprehension of an essentially bicultural world. To understand it, he had to look in two directions at the same time: to his own family and people, and to the dominant white community that surrounded him.

As he watched his white contemporaries, he confronted an example of one of the small wonders of history—the stability and perseverance of the traditions of childhood. Undisturbed by distance and political upheaval, the sons and daughters of Georgia and South Carolina planters went on playing the same games that their great-great-grandparents had played in the streets of London or Edinburgh. The black children from the "quarters" stood and watched, or perhaps they were allowed to play, too.

The group of games in this section, then, might be considered a kind of platform upon which Euro-American and Afro-American children met during our country's growing up. Originally I put them together simply because they did not seem to fit anywhere else, and I had titled this section "Miscellaneous" until I realized that the term is inaccurate. There is a logical relationship here; these are the singing games that hold closest to British origins. (Other singing games in other sections can be traced back to England, too, but through a more complicated path.)

Mrs. Jones, by the way, did not know what to call these particular games herself. She referred to various ones of them at various times as "plays," "singing plays," and "little what-nots." I have used the second of her titles, although the third reflects her point of view more accurately, I think.

Interestingly, these are always the favorite plays among white students I have taught; this is, I believe, because of their emphasis upon *form* rather than *style*. Mrs. Jones, too, appreciated this quality; the ceremonial tracing out of pattern which is so important in these games deeply appealed to her. She referred to them over and over as "*beautiful* plays" and, intuitively striking at the heart of the matter, would say

Oh, I like that. There's so much meaning *to it. . . .*

Green, Green, the Crab Apple Tree

It's a play . . . I'll tell you how it go. You stand in a ring and just go round and you call different ones' names, and they turn back, you know. . . . They're flowers, see? . . .

I first played this game with Mrs. Jones and the Sea Islanders on a bright morning in my living room, climbing over dogs and recording equipment to do so. It was a strange experience to "turn back my head" on the friendly clutter of my own life, while my friends and I moved through the ancient pattern, originally a child's reenactment of a mourning rite. In most of the English-speaking world, "Green, Green, the Crab Apple Tree" is called "Green Gravel" or, sometimes, "Green Graves."

Actually it is a ceremonial dance, rather than a game; the pace should be moderate and the movements smooth. While I was learning the tune, Mrs. Hillary joined in with a "tenor" part of such brilliant and intense dissonance that I have transcribed it here. Though the game is always played quite cheerfully, when Mrs. Hillary's vocal part is added, this little fragment of man's remote past becomes solemn and mysterious.

FORM: A ring of children holding hands. All walk in a counterclockwise circle while all sing.

LEAD VOICE	GROUP VOICE	ACTION
	Green, green, the crab apple tree, Where the grass grows so deep.	Children, holding hands, circle in a walking step in time to the singing.
	Miss	
Emma,		
	Miss	
Emma,		
	Your true lover is dead. He wrote you a letter To turn back your head.	On "turn," child whose name has been sung drops hands, turns halfway around with back to the center of the ring, and joins hands again, and the circling movement continues until all the players have been called.

Green, Green, the Crab Apple Tree

Words and music by Bessie Jones; collected and edited with new material by Alan Lomax. TRO—

Johnny Cuckoo

The children are in a line and one person walks up and he be's one Johnny Cuckoo. And he sings back and forth and takes one and takes him back with him. Then there's two Johnny Cuckoos. . . .

The ancient British game "Three Dukes A-Riding" is a courtship play in which an increasing number of "dukes" come to choose their brides from a line of young maidens, in what may be a reflection of marriage customs between clans in old Britain. Both British and American writers describe it as a line play, with the parallel lines of maidens and dukes advancing and retreating, looking "contemptuously and criticizingly" at each other as they sing "You are too black and blowsy" and "We are quite as good as you, sirs" before they finally join forces.

The Sea Islanders don't bother with "contemptuous and criticizing looks"; they simply turn their backs and "switch" their hips in their opponents' faces. (The hip-switching motion is achieved by standing with the legs together and bending one knee forward while the other goes back into a locked position; alternate knees for the other side.) Further, the plot of Mrs. Jones's version no longer concerns coquetry and courtship but the choosing of "soldiers"; the phrase "You are too black and dirty" is scarcely part of the language of love.

In play, however, this is an uproariously good-humored game and one of the favorites of both adults and children. Both sides get to dramatize hostility in a very down-to-earth fashion; and even though children are used to having rude remarks made about their personal appearance, the ones I have seen playing this game get absolutely enormous satisfaction out of being able to answer back, for once, "I am just as clean as you are!"

FORM: Line of children singing and clapping a single offbeat clap. One player (Johnny Cuckoo) faces the line.

ALL VOICES*	ACTION
Here comes one Johnny Cuckoo, Cuckoo, Cuckoo. Here comes one Johnny Cuckoo On a cold and stormy night.	Single player approaches line and walks back and forth inspecting the "troops."

What did you come for,
Come for, come for,
What did you come for
On a cold and stormy night?

I come for me (We come for us)
a soldier,
Soldier, a soldier,
I come for me (We come for us)
a soldier
On a cold and stormy night.

(Slight increase of speed, begin
double offbeat clap)
You look too black and dirty,
Dirty, dirty,
You look too black and dirty
On a cold and stormy night.

All players in the line turn their backs on Johnny Cuckoo and switch their hips at him, turning to face him on the last word.

I am (We are) just as clean as
you are,
You are, you are,
I am (We are) just as clean as
you are
On a cold and stormy night.

Center player turns his back on the line and switches his hips at them, turning back and selecting another player on the last word.

Now here comes two Johnny
Cuckoos, etc.

Game is repeated with two Johnny Cuckoos, at the end of which the original selects another player to repeat the play with three, and so on.

* Though this is a game in which the conversation switches back and forth from the line to Johnny Cuckoo, the Sea Islanders sing all the verses together all the way through. I suspect this is just because they enjoy singing the song in harmony.

Johnny Cuckoo

Written and adapted by Bessie Jones; collected and edited by Alan Lomax.

Oh Green Fields, Roxie

This play moves, and just like you're hearing it go now, you move with it. . . . You got to move with it, so you can really be stirred.

Mrs. Jones's passionate remark was caused by her catching sight of a player tramping casually, and out of rhythm, into the center of the ring. If you do "clap it right and play it *right*," as Mrs. Jones points out, this little play really *does* move.

It is also an excellent example of the Afro-American way with a British song. Its early ancestor was a delicate little verse to a skipping rhythm:

Green grow the rushes, oh,
Green grow the rushes, oh,
He who will my true love be
Come and sit by the side of me!

In Mrs. Jones's neighborhood, the breathy word "rushes" became the explosive and crackling "Roxie!"; the tempo changed from a skip to a strut. When accompanied by a solid offbeat clap, this can be one of the most jazzily rhythmic of all Mrs. Jones's plays.

FORM: Ring of children standing and clapping. In the middle of the ring is a chair with a player sitting in it. The "caller," who leads the singing, stands by the chair.

LEAD VOICE	GROUP VOICE	ACTION
Oh green fields,		All players clapping.
	Roxie,	
Oh green fields,		
	Roxie,	
Tell me who you love,		Caller leans over to player in
	Roxie,	the chair, who whispers the
Tell me who you love,		name of another player to the
	Roxie,	caller.
(Lead voice solo)		
Oh, Miss (Mabel) your name is called,		Caller sings the whispered name.
Come take a seat right side your love,		Player called struts to chair, shakes hands with player in
Shake his hand and let him go,		chair,

Don't let him sit in that chair
no more.

and sits down. First player dances back to the ring and the game is repeated without pause.

Oh Green Fields, Roxie

Go In and Out the Window

This is another example of how fortunate Americans are to have British melody and African rhythm combining into their national musical language. To anyone who has doggedly skipped (or trudged when the teacher wasn't looking) through this play on a hot asphalt playground, the Sea Islanders' swing through this old chestnut will be a revelation. Be sure and give it a solid offbeat clap.

Mrs. Jones says that "to measure your love" you take a piece of paper (about the size of a small envelope), hold it by diagonal corners up to the breast of your partner, "measuring" by raising and lowering your hands in a seesawing motion, so that first one corner is up, then the other.

The refrain "As we have came today" is probably a variation of the line "As we have gained the day" from the widespread version which begins, "We're marching round the levee." Grammarians may make their own selection.

FORM: Children standing in a ring, holding hands with arms high to form arches. Drop hands and clap after first verse. One player in center, who has a piece of paper or handkerchief in hand (see above).

ALL VOICES EXCEPT CENTER PLAYER	ACTION
Go in and out the window, Go in and out the window, Go in and out the window, As we have came today.	Center player walks, to time, out of ring through one arch, back in through next, and so on.
I kneel because I love you, I kneel because I love you, I kneel because I love you As we have came today.	Center player kneels before the player he has reached at beginning of verse; no choice allowed.
I measure my love to show you, I measure my love to show you, I measure my love to show you As we have came today.	Center player "measures love" as described above; this action must be done to time.

Shake hands before I leave you,
Shake hands before I leave you,
Shake hands before I leave you
As we have came today.

Center player and partner shake hands, also to time.

Center player and partner change places and play continues with new center player, who takes the "measure" with him.

Go In and Out the Window

Draw Me a Bucket of Water

Back up to where I was brought up at, we had big huge wells with two buckets on it. You know how to draw up that way? Bring up one bucket and carry down another one, you know, so you won't lose no time. . . . And so anyway, the wells what we had, the top wouldn't be on it—you know, just an open well—and they made a song about that. The frog would get in our well, you see, because it didn't have no top on it. And snakes would get in our well, but we'd shake 'em out or fish 'em out or get 'em out because you sure couldn't dreen the well and wash 'em out. And we had to drink the water. . . .

Mrs. Jones's imaginative explanation accounts for the combination here of two traditional games of British origin ("Draw a Bucket of Water"and "Frog in the Middle"). Her version differs from other descriptions I have seen in the method of play and perhaps is closer to dance than game. It was a strong favorite with all students at the summer workshop.

The play is unique in Mrs. Jones's repertoire in that it requires an exact number of players. Two couples stand in the form of a square, holding hands with their opposite partners; each couple sways back and forth pulling their arms in a seesawing motion. At the phrase "Go under, sister Sally," the couple whose arms are on top of the cross raises arms to make an arch on one side only. The player on that side ducks under and thus is the "one in the bunch"; she does *not* drop her partner's hands.

The verse is repeated until the opposite partner of the "one in the bunch" ducks under the alternate raised arms to make "two in the bunch." On the third repetition, the inside couple raises their clasped hands to arch so that one of the outside couples can come under. After the fourth repetition, all players will find that they are standing with their arms twined around each other. They then dance around with a "buzz step" through the first singing of the "Frog in the Bucket" verse, and "step it down" the second time.

The major directions to remember here are neither to drop hands nor to twist or cross them; the pattern is extremely simple to execute (though difficult to describe). Emotionally, there is an enormous satisfaction in completing this lovely weaving figure.

FORM: Four children standing in a square; each holds hands with the opposite partner. (See diagram.) A's and B's arms are on top of the cross. Do *not* drop hands until last verse.

ALL VOICES	ACTION
Draw me a bucket of water For my oldest daughter. We got none in the bunch, We're all out the bunch.	Players sway forward and back in a seesawing motion.
You go under, sister Sally.	Player D ducks under arch formed by right arm of player A and left arm of player B.
Draw me a bucket of water For my oldest daughter. We got one in the bunch And three out the bunch.	Swaying motion continues; players C and D do *not* drop hands; neither do A and B.
You go under, sister Sally.	Player C ducks under arch made by left arm of player A and right arm of player B.
Draw me a bucket of water For my oldest daughter. We got two in the bunch And two out the bunch.	Swaying continues, though C and D, still holding hands, have to confine their motion.
You go under, sister Sally.	Player A ducks under arch made by right arm of player C and left of player D.
Draw me a bucket of water For my oldest daughter. We got three in the bunch And one out the bunch.	Swaying continues, though space is highly constricted.
You go under, sister Sally.	Player B ducks under arch made by raised left arm of player C and right of player D.
Frog in the bucket and I can't get him out. (Repeat four times.)	With arms entwined, still holding the original hands, players dance round in a circle, using the buzz step.
Frog in the bucket and I can't get him out. (Repeat four times.)	Players drop hands and rejoin them in a simple circle and "step it down."

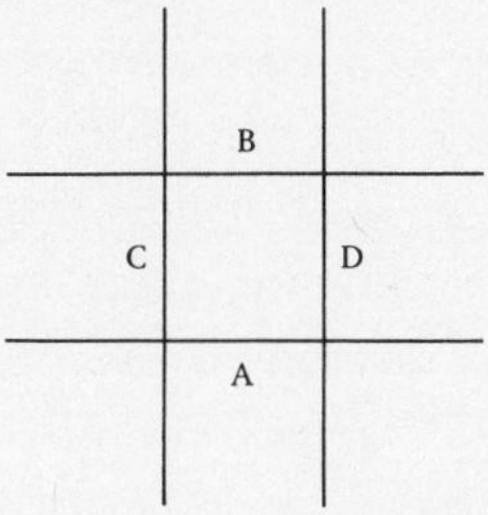

B

C D

A

Draw Me a Bucket of Water

Nana, Thread Needle

This is a beautiful play. . . . This play shows you how people can borrow from you and never pay it back. And when they say, "I'm going to wind up this bunkum," it means, "I'm going to wind up this borrowing." I like this because there's so much to it, there's so much meaning in it. . . .

This is another combination of several British plays widespread, in various forms, through the Caribbean area as well as the Southern United States. It is one of the most satisfying of all Mrs. Jones's plays, but to really enjoy it remember that it is a *play*, a ceremonial tracing of pattern, not a *game*.

Mrs. Jones was quite firm about the phrase "thread needle." When players sang "thread *the* needle," she remarked, "We didn't know nothing about no thread *the* needle; it's *thread needle*." I do not know why this was so important to her.

To play, a group of children stand in line; they hold hands throughout the entire game. They should be arranged roughly by height, from the tallest to the shortest (here indicated from A to Z). The two players on the ends of the line hold a brief conversation:

A (tallest): Neighbor, neighbor, lend me your hatchet.
Z (shortest): Neighbor, neighbor, step and get it.

A then starts out at a steady walking pace and leads through the arch made by the hands of B and C. This forces B to turn under her own arm, a movement called in some games "wringing the dishrag." (If the players do not hold hands tightly but allow the turning player's hand to rotate naturally, she will revolve back to her original position without a sprained wrist.) Player A continues leading the marching line around and through the arch between players C and D, and so on through each pair of arms in a gradually enlarging concentric spiral, while singing:

LEAD VOICE (PLAYER A)	GROUP VOICE	ACTION
Nana,		(As described above)
	Thread needle.	
Nana,		
	Thread needle.	

I wants my needle.
Thread needle.
I lost my needle.
Thread needle.
My gold-eyed needle.
Thread needle.
It's mama's needle.
Thread needle.

The lead singer's lines are improvised, depending on choice and the length of the line; she may return to "nana," which Mrs. Jones says means "mama," whenever she likes.

When the space Y and Z has been "sewn" through and the line returned to its original form, there is another conversation.

> Z (shortest): Neighbor, neighbor, send me my hatchet.
> A (tallest): Neighbor, neighbor, I ain't got it.

Z then starts skipping out, leading her end of the line around A, who stands still. Z (who has to be in pretty good condition) continues skipping around and around until the whole line is wound up in a concentric spiral, like a tight watch spring, around A. The players do *not* drop hands, and must move with each other; there should be no pulling apart. While this circling movement is going on, all players sing, repeating over and over:

> Going to wind up-a this bunkum, bunkum,
> Wind up-a this bunkum.
> Wind up-a this bunkum, bunkum,
> Wind up-a this bunkum.

When this movement is finished, and you have, as Mrs. Jones puts it, "nothing but a big ball of children," all the players jump up and down together, singing:

> Going to shake down-a this bunkum, bunkum,
> Shake down-a this bunkum.
> Shake down-a this bunkum, bunkum,
> Shake down-a this bunkum.

After everyone is "shaken down" sufficiently (the verse may be repeated as often as desired), Z turns back and retraces her skip, leading the line back to the starting position, while singing:

Going to unwind-a this bunkum, bunkum,
Unwind-a this bunkum.
Unwind-a this bunkum, bunkum,
Unwind-a this bunkum. . . .

Nana, Thread Needle

5:
Ring Plays

And the children all stand in a ring . . .

The notion of a ring has always had a quality of magic; during play it is, literally, a "charmed circle." It includes and excludes at the same time. It surrounds and enfolds while it walls off and repels. Inside a ring, within its bounds, you are safe from what is "outside"; you are in a special world in which you may be either king or prisoner. The ring is without gap or weakness—perhaps strength is its underlying symbolic quality.

The strength of a ring is in its construction. Since it has neither beginning nor end, there can be no ranking of its parts—no strong or weak, big or little. In the old fairy tales, the giving of a ring often is a token of union and a pledge of constancy, but sometimes the magical ring has another function: it makes the wearer invisible. And so with the individual. When you are part of a ring, you are just that—part of a ring. There are no head and foot couples, no captains, no opposing ranks. It is the signal form of democracy.

Given the basic construction of a ring, there are many ways in which dramatic or symbolic play can develop. Its strength can be attacked from the outside or from the inside. It may develop gaps which must be filled, as in the many forms of "Drop the Handkerchief." Gates may open to allow players to leave the circle and make a venture into the outside world, or it may expand concentrically into two circles. It can become a wheel, or two wheels, which can rotate together or in opposing motion.

Such basic circular play forms, as well as many others, have been the historic property of both children and adults in all times and all places. It seems likely, then, that the ring plays of black Americans are revisions and combinations of both European and African games and ceremonials.

But as I have already mentioned, there are lots of things that can happen inside and outside of a ring. In thinking about Mrs. Jones's repertoire of circle games, there is one set of actions so frequent that it seems, both to me and to Mrs. Jones, a special category. It is this particular set of actions which are referred to as "ring play" throughout this book.

The "ring play," as the term is used here, consists of a group standing in a circle, clapping, singing, and musically supporting a single central character who acts out his own brief drama on center stage, as it were, before he chooses another to take his place. Mrs. Jones puts it more succinctly:

One gets in the middle of the ring and they all clap and sing, you see. . . . And it go on until you get to each one. . . .

The center player in the ring play, then, stands alone to make his statement by dance or "acting," usually within the context of courtship play. But this is a different kind of courtship than that dramatized by British children, for instance, who choose partners and end by singing:

Now, you are married, you must be good
And make your husband chop the wood.

The ring player makes his statement of romantic availability all by himself; at the end of his turn, he picks out not so much a partner as a successor. There is little, if any, paired or coupled action.

The emotional climate of ring play is humorous, if not uproarious. The Islanders clearly thought the ring plays were the most fun of all. They provided an opportunity for the hottest dancing, the most ridiculous miming, the most exaggerated horseplay. As I watched, it seemed to me that the ring play was the moment of individuation—

for the child, the culmination of his learning skills, the announcement of his separation from the family.

For one thing, the usual family taboos and prohibitions are suspended. Black children are not encouraged in "real life" to "put on airs" or to flaunt themselves publicly. In the ring play, they may strut and tease, flirt and wiggle, while everybody claps for them. In Mrs. Jones's comment on "Soup, Soup" you can find her own recognition of the pleasure she found in being able to break the rules, to act out the forbidden.

But the separation is not complete. The ring player is not alone; he is accompanied by singing, and the singers make constant contact with him. "What can you do?" they ask him. "Show me your motion!" Usually, however, the group simply comments on the action, rather than directing it. "Way go, Lily!" they sing, as Lily flies across the ring. Or they make remarks about the player's person—"Oh, she's neat in the waist, and she's pretty in the face."

Adult Negroes in Southern rural churches will give just such vocal support as they respond to the prayers and testimonies of church members who feel the call to speak. To use their own lovely phrase, they will "bear up" their minister as he preaches, just as the trumpet and trombone fill in musically under the clarinet solo in the New Orleans jazz ensemble. In the ring play, a further extension of the principle of antiphony, or responsiveness, begins to be plain: the individual is always supported by a nondirective group and, just as important, he comes out of and eventually returns to that group.

The Islanders found it almost incomprehensible that I wanted an explanation of the ring plays before I would try them myself. "Come on, it's just a little play!" they would urge. The power of the ring, for them, was unbroken. They *knew* that the surrounding group would support the shy or the awkward just as strongly as it would the bold or the graceful, and that no dancer would get more or less time than any other. For them, the ring play seemed to be the ultimate opportunity for personal reassurance, for feeling the warmth and support of a tight-locked and indestructible circle within which they could act out all their feelings without any fear of rejection or shame. And so it must be, too, for the black child making his first steps into the larger world beyond the family.

For me, though—and, I suspect, for most of the other white

players—the taking of the center of the ring was a kind of horrible, publicly stated moment of truth. I didn't have many motions, to begin with, and those I had seemed all wrong. It is, perhaps, one of the finest ironies of the American dilemma that the isolated minority should be able to speak among its friends so much more freely than the dominant majority.

However, due to the patience and enthusiasm of the Islanders, I did eventually begin to get some of the feeling of ring play. Here are some of its working principles, many of which, because of the central importance of the form, are applicable to plays not included in this section.

1. There may be almost any number of players, odd or even, though it is difficult to work with less than six or more than ten or twelve. On one occasion when we had thirty players, I suggested to Mrs. Jones that we use two central figures, moving in different parts of the ring. Though she agreed and I felt the arrangement worked out well, it was obviously not a normal or comfortable procedure for Mrs. Jones. There should be only *one* player in the ring; her solution, as I realized later, would have been to divide into two separate groups.

2. The circle players always sing, clap, and usually "step it down" a little as well, shifting their weight from side to side in the foot move described at the beginning of Chapter 2: Clapping Plays (p. 20). This is *not* the dance step also known as "stepping it down" but the ordinary physical accompaniment to *clapping* that serves, here, both to keep the rhythm solid and to keep each player physically tensed and ready to take his turn. Since each center player chooses the one to follow him, the other players' turns may come at the end of any run-through.

3. These are *plays,* not games. The center player is an actor and should "act out" each phrase of the song that describes him. For instance, in "East Coast Line" the center player may strut or dance inside the circle through the first five lines of the song, but should act out the lines "she's neat in the waist and she's pretty in the face" even if, as Mrs. Jones remarked, "she's got a big old whomper like me."

4. The center player is also a *dancer,* and walks (dances) to time from the moment he comes out of the surrounding ring until he returns to it. When he chooses the next dancer, the choice must al-

ways "come out right with the music." If he misjudges, he must choose the player he can reach on time.

5. Play is continuous. While the moment when an action should *begin* is indicated by underlining the appropriate word in the song text, the action should be carried on until the next direction is given. And at the end of one round of play, when a new center player takes over, play continues without pause until everyone has had a turn.

6. "Lead singer" and "center player" are, of course, different roles. The lead singer may be *any* player with a strong voice and some extra energy; when the time comes for the singer to take a turn as center player, another voice will often take over the lead role. Thus the center player position changes with each run-through of the play, while the lead singer may continue through the entire play session, or, as her voice grows tired, a fresher voice may spontaneously take over.

7. Some of the plays included in this section could have been placed elsewhere; actually, Mrs. Jones called some of them different things at different times. Man and his works are simply too diverse to be neat. However, to the player, the problem of categorization doesn't matter much, except in the subtle area of how a game "feels." Most of the workshop students, probably for emotional reasons, seemed to find the "pure" ring plays, such as "Soup, Soup" or "East Coast Line," the most difficult; they tended to prefer (find easier) those plays which are closer to dance, such as "Way Down Yonder in the Brickyard" or "Steal Up, Young Lady." All the plays, however, call on basically the same *physical* skills, though "Way Go, Lily" has the simplest movement pattern and "Uncle Jessie" the most complicated. Because of this cultural complication, I have made no effort to arrange the items in this section according to difficulty, and players will simply have to decide for themselves which are "hard" and which are "easy."

Little Johnny Brown

You got to time it right to play it right. . . .

This seems to me to be a very old play; I have not found it reported anywhere else. The specific nature of the early part of the action makes it very popular with children, though the later (and more characteristic) part is more difficult.

Mrs. Jones's concern with timing showed here with her insistence, during play, that the "comfort" (comforter) be spread down on the fourth line of the verse, so that there would be no awkward time gap to be filled in by the center player. The folding of the comfort (usually represented by a bandanna or man's large handkerchief) is ceremonial: one corner is folded to the center, then the opposite corner, then the side corners in turn, leaving a much reduced square of cloth. The player walks around to a different corner of the handkerchief and stoops down each time he makes a fold.

FORM: Ring of players standing and clapping; one player in the center.

GROUP AND LEAD VOICES TOGETHER	ACTION
Little Johnny Brown, Spread your comfort down.	Center player walks around in middle of the ring.
Little Johnny Brown, Spread your comfort down.	Center player spreads handkerchief out in middle of the floor.

LEAD VOICE	GROUP VOICE	ACTION
Fold one corner,	Johnny Brown.	Center player folds one corner of handkerchief to middle.
Fold another corner,	Johnny Brown.	Center player folds opposite corner as above.
Fold another corner,	Johnny Brown.	Center player folds side corner.
Fold another corner,	Johnny Brown.	Center player folds last corner.
Take it to your lover, Take it to your lover,	Johnny Brown. Johnny Brown.	Center player dances over to player in ring. He must face partner by the last "lover."
Show her your motion,	Johnny Brown.	Center player "makes his motion" (see p. 46).

Show her your motion,
Johnny Brown.

Lope like a buzzard,
Johnny Brown.

Center player does "buzzard lope" (see p. 45).

Lope like a buzzard,
Johnny Brown.

Give it to your lover,
Johnny Brown.

Center player hands folded handkerchief to his partner, who then goes to center ring and play begins over without pause.

Give it to your lover,
Johnny Brown.

Give it to your lover,
Johnny Brown.

Little Johnny Brown

East Coast Line

We thought Jacksonville was the magic city of the world, you know, because we heard so much talk of it. And it was on the East Coast Line. . . .

She eats syrup by the gallon, you know; she eats meat by the pound. And by eating all that, she looks good; she's neat in the waist and pretty in the face. . . . She eats bread by the pone—that's corn-bread you pat out with your hands. Some peoples make up little bitty pones about as big as your fist, but we used to make up them big old ravish pones; they're really good. . . .

Children are all bottomless pits, and their legs are hollow; but the children of Emancipation sing about how *pretty* you can be if you have good food.

FORM: Ring of children standing and clapping, one player in the center.

LEAD VOICE	GROUP VOICE	ACTION
Way down yonder,		Center player walks (struts)
	Hey,	around inside the ring.
On the East Coast Line,		
	Hey,	
They eat syrup by the gallon,		
	Hey,	
They eat meat by the pound,		
	Hey,	
They eating bread by the pone,		
	Hey,	
And she's neat in the waist,		Center player mimes being
	Hey,	neat in the waist and pretty in
And she's pretty in the face,		the face.
	Hey,	
And if I were you,		Center player "struts" around
	Hey,	inside the ring.
And you were me,		
	Hey,	
I would stop right still,		Center player stops in front
	Hey,	of prospective partner.
And shake it back,		Center player switches hips.

Shake it to the east,
Shake it to the west,
Shake it to the very one
That you love the best.

Center player leaves ring; partner takes her place.

East Coast Line

*A minor chord (a, c, e) used throughout on word "Hey."

Sir Mister Brown

In this play when you dance together you say what kind of lady she is and what kind of person you're dancing with. You claim *she's that way—you know she's not that kind. . . .*

The workshop group persisted in singing *both* the second and fourth lines of this tune with the descending cadence, ending on the tonic note. Mrs. Jones, stating plainly her feelings about the interrelationship of text and tune, said, "The first time you say it, you're *asking* for her—Sir Mister Brown?" (singing unfinished cadence: B A G B). "The second time, you've done paid for her and you *got* her—Sir Mister *Brown!*" And she ended triumphantly on the tonic note of G.

The Islanders had a lot of fun with this rather satiric lyric, acting out obsequiousness during the first two lines and so on.

FORM: Ring of children standing, one player in the center.

LEAD VOICE AND GROUP VOICE	ACTION
Mister Brown, Mister Brown, I come to court your daughter, Sir Mister Brown. Mister Brown, Mister Brown, I'll give you a dollar and a quarter,	Center player walks around inside ring.
Sir Mister Brown.	Center player stands in front of partner.

Start offbeat clap (lead singer and group)

LEAD VOICE	GROUP VOICE	ACTION
Fly round, my lady,	Sir Mister Brown.	Center player and partner "jump for joy."
That lady's going to meet you,	Sir Mister Brown.	
That big-eyed lady,	Sir Mister Brown.	
That cockeyed lady,	Sir Mister Brown.	
That one-legged lady,	Sir Mister Brown.	
That bowlegged lady,	Sir Mister Brown.	

Now Sir Mister Brown	Now Sir Mister Brown.	Center player joins ring; partner moves into center and play repeats.

Sir Mister Brown

Way Down Yonder, Sometimes

In this ring play, an account of the doings of magical animals and the courtship feats of human beings is continually punctuated by the chorus's sardonic remark "Sometimes." The tune, when sung and clapped with strong rhythm, will give you an idea of how interesting only four notes can be.

FORM: Ring of players, not holding hands; one center player.

LEAD VOICE	CHORUS VOICE	ACTION
Way down yonder,	Sometimes,	Center player walks (struts) around the ring.
Below the log,	Sometimes,	
Wild geese are holl'ring,	Sometimes,	
Ganders trot,	Sometimes,	
Bullfrog marry,	Sometimes,	
His mother-in-law,	Sometimes,	
Now let's get on board,	Sometimes,	Center player stands in front of chosen partner.
I'm going to ball that jack,	Sometimes,	Center player balls the jack (see p. 44).
Until my honey comes back,	Sometimes,	
I want to rear back, Jack,	Sometimes,	Center player (and partner) lean back.
And get a hump in my back,	Sometimes,	Center player (and partner) hunch shoulders.
I'm going over here,	Sometimes,	Center player takes partner's hand and turns her into center of the circle, taking
Goin' to get my pal,	Sometimes.	her place in the ring. Play continues with the new center player.

Way Down Yonder, Sometimes

Soup, Soup

I like that part about they ain't but the one thing that I dislike. You see in the old times people taught you how to do, and they didn't like you to do things like putting on airs or posing for mens, but they'd yet get down to the raw thing and ball the jack! I thought that was so cute. . . .

The Negro rural community has had its own share of conflict over standards of proper behavior. The whole area of dance has been especially tense because of the direct conflict between ancient African cultural patterns, in which dance is a routine part of almost all human activity, and European Protestantism, in which dance is considered by all except a few dissenting sects to be both worldly and potentially lustful.

On the level of children's activity, both white and black communities have attempted to regard singing games as *playing*, not *dancing*, and therefore allowable, without many restrictions, to the young. The children of both communities have, in turn, fashioned their pastimes in direct celebration of the adult world they saw around them. In this context one can see the irony that Mrs. Jones points out. How pleasant it is to be allowed to demonstrate explicitly and exactly just what it is you disapprove of.

FORM: Ring of players, not holding hands, one player in the center.

LEAD VOICE	GROUP VOICE	ACTION
Way down yonder,		Center player walks around inside ring.
	Soup, soup.	
Below the moon,		
	Soup, soup.	
I got a letter,		
	Soup, soup.	
From Alma Stone,		
	Soup, soup.	
They <u>ain't</u> but the one thing,		Center player picks partner and stands in front of him.
	Soup, soup.	
That I dislike,		
	Soup, soup.	
That's <u>putting</u> on airs,		Center player mimes "putting on airs."
	Soup, soup.	
And <u>balling</u> that jack.		Center player balls the jack.

Soup, soup.

That buzzard soup, Soup, soup. — Center player and partner ball the jack to each other.

That rabbit soup, Soup, soup.

That monkey soup, Soup, soup.

That gopher soup, Soup, soup.

That elephant soup, Soup, soup. — Partner moves out to center of ring and center player takes her place; play repeats with new center player.

Soup, Soup

Punchinello

Old Sue, she's going to have to do just about what Sally done. . . .

Apparently this European singing game entered the American game repertoire around the turn of the century in the form of a rather awkward translation that was printed widely in school music texts:

> Ho! look at me,
> Punchinello, funny fellow.
> Ho! look at me,
> Punchinello, funny do.

The form of the dance—a ring with a center player—immediately attracted the children of the Negro community, who then set about remaking "Punchinello" into a completely comfortable play. Mrs. Jones remarked that she had left out "some of the verses about 'who do you choose' and like that because you don't need them."

Instead of the original second and fourth lines, Mrs. Jones sings "Punchinello, follow Sally," and "Punchinello, follow Sue." These phrases may require further changing; as the remark under the title indicates, Mrs. Jones feels a little concern over Sue's presence. (There should be *one* person in the center in a ring play, and on rare occasions, two. Three—Punchinello, Sally, *and* Sue—is certainly too many.) Los Angeles children I have heard playing this popular game don't bother with Sally and Sue at all; they sing "Punchinello, forty-seven" and "Punchinello, forty-two."

Perhaps because of exposure to the textbook version of this play, the students in the workshop were unusually square with this tune, insisting on clapping on the downbeat instead of the offbeat. In an effort to improve the rhythm, Emma Ramsey broke into a fast rumba-like clapping pattern (transcribed in the music over the words "I can do it too"). This, combined with Mrs. Jones's steady offbeat baritone clap, certainly completed the transformation of this somewhat galumphing European dance into one of the most swinging of the Sea Islanders' plays.

FORM: Ring of children standing and clapping; center player in the middle of the circle.

LEAD VOICE	GROUP VOICE	ACTION
Look who is here,		Center player walks
	Punchinello, follow Sally,	around inside ring.
Look who is here,		
	Punchinello, follow Sue.	Center player stops in front of chosen partner.
What can you do?		Center player "makes
	Punchinello, follow Sally,	his motion."
What can you do?		
	Punchinello, follow Sue.	
Well, I can do it too,		Partner imitates center
	Punchinello, follow Sally,	player's "motion."
I can do it too,		
	Punchinello, follow Sue.	Partner takes center ring and game starts over while first center player joins the ring.

Mrs. Jones says that if it's a large ring and you're getting tired, you can sing "We can do it too" and all the ring players can then imitate the dance step of the last center player. This, however, will end the play; the pattern has been destroyed.

Punchinello

Little Sally Walker

If you got something to move, you can move it. If you ain't got nothing to move, you can't move nothing. . . .

For another example of how a European game can be changed into ring play, here is "Little Sally Walker," long a favorite among British and American children. It is a very old play. In what are perhaps the oldest versions, little Sally's last name is "Water" instead of "Walker" and she is "crying for a young man." Some writers suggest that this play may have grown out of purification ceremonies in ancient British marriage rites.

In sin-conscious early America, however, "Little Sally Walker" became a brief drama about the joys of release from shame; black children undoubtedly learned it from their white neighbors. Mrs. Jones knew three distinct versions. Version One, which she sings in a flowing and unsyncopated style markedly unlike her usual vigorous rhythm and which she says is "the old way to play it," is the one most similar to white versions I have heard. The concluding stanzas of all three versions seem to be Negro additions. "Flying," even to the east and the west, is certainly a less emphatic expression of happiness than "jumping for joy," "shaking it," or "letting your backbone slip." (Mrs. Jones remarked reassuringly one day, "That letting your backbone slip is *good* for you—it'll make you souple all over!")

VERSION ONE

FORM: Ring of children standing; center player sits or kneels in the middle of the ring.

ALL VOICES EXCEPT CENTER PLAYER	ACTION
Little Sally Walker, Sitting in a saucer, Crying and a-weeping Over all she has done.	Center player puts head in hands as though crying.
Rise, Sally, rise. Wipe out your eyes. Fly to the east, Sally,	Center player stands; wipes eyes; arms outstretched and waving, walks to right;
Fly to the west, Sally, Fly to the very one that you love the best.	as above walks to left; as above, goes to face chosen partner.

(Begin strong offbeat clap) * Now Miss Sally, won't you jump for joy, Jump for joy, jump for joy. Now Miss Sally, won't you jump for joy, And now, Miss Sally, won't you bow.	Center player and partner jump for joy.
	Center player bows; partner takes place in center while first Little Sally joins the ring.

VERSION TWO

This version is sung at a faster tempo with strong syncopation throughout, as well as a decided offbeat clap. The movements are stylized and should be rigidly held to time with the singing. The words accompanying the actions are underlined.

FORM: Ring of children standing and clapping. Center player sits in middle.

ALL VOICES EXCEPT CENTER PLAYER	ACTION
Little Sally Walker, Sitting in a saucer, Crying and a-weeping over all she have done.	Center player, face in hands, mimes crying.
Oh, rise up on your feet, Oh, wipe your cheeks, Oh, turn to the east, Oh, turn to the west, Oh, turn to the very one that you love the best.	Center player stands; wipes cheeks—R L R; turns right step, step, step; turns left—step, step, step; turns to find chosen partner.
Oh, shake it to the east, Oh, shake it to the west, Oh, shake it to the very one that you love the best.	Hands on hips, switch hips—R L R; as above—L R L; as above, alternate hip-switching; change place with partner on last word. Partner becomes next Sally Walker.

* Mrs. Jones says you can sing "Now let me see how you jump for joy" at the end of the play so the whole ring can dance at one time.

VERSION THREE

Mrs. Jones's third version, which she learned last and does, indeed, seem more modern, is identical with Version One through the words "Fly to the very one that you love the best," though the tune is sung faster and she claps throughout. The following lines then occur:

> Now put your hand on your hip
> And let your backbone slip.
> Shake it to the east,
> Shake it to the west,
> Shake it to the very one that you love the best.

Little Sally Walker

(version 1)

Little Sally Walker

(version 2)

(version 3)

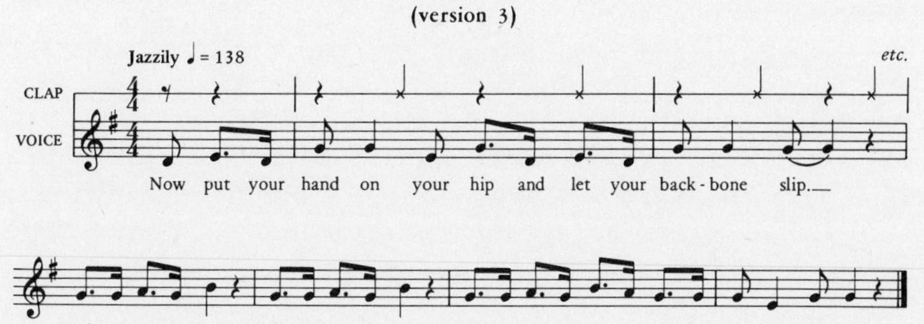
Jazzily ♩ = 138
etc.
CLAP
VOICE
Now put your hand on your hip and let your back-bone slip.

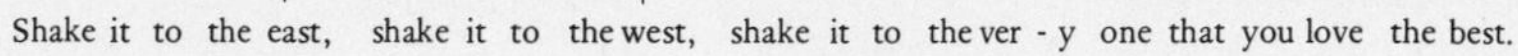
Shake it to the east, shake it to the west, shake it to the ver-y one that you love the best.

Uncle Jessie

I tell you what this means, it means a boss man coming across the field. Sometimes he's feeling good, and sometimes he's not. Sometimes he's worried; maybe sometimes he done lost and sometimes he done gained, and I know how he feels. . . . But he still walked like a big-stepping man; he stepped big like he made a thousand dollars. . . . But sometimes he's feeling good and sometimes he's not. . . .

"Uncle Jessie" seems to be one of the oldest of the Islanders' plays; one evidence of its age is the mention of love and power charms in the form of salt, garlic, and onion. The formal dancing by the central partners puts it almost into the category of dance rather than ring play; in action, actually, it feels like a cross between the two.

During the chorus, which may be sung either "Step, Uncle Jessie" or "Walk, Uncle Jessie," the center players dance together as a couple. They hold hands in a skaters' waltz position and either strut or slide in a two-step rhythm:

Step,	Uncle	Jes -	sie,	step,		step	
R	L slide	R	rest	L	R slide	L	rest

When the partners have two-stepped to the inside limits of the ring, they reverse their direction by turning toward each other and shifting the relation of their arms while continuing to hold hands as before. As Mrs. Jones puts it,

When you go to turn, you don't have to wheel; you just turn like you're sawing. It's beautiful; you step and move together, just right with the song. . . .

FORM: Ring of players standing and clapping; one player in the center.

LEAD VOICE AND/OR GROUP VOICE	ACTION
Now, here comes Uncle Jessie, Coming through the field With his horse and buggy	Center player walks around in center of ring (in time with the music) acting out Uncle Jessie.
And I know just how he feels. (The next verse may be added now or substituted for the first verse.)	Stops in front of partner (one of the ring players) on the last word of either verse.

Here comes Uncle Jessie,
He's looking very sad.
He's lost his cotton and corn
And everything he had.

Step, Uncle Jessie, step, step, Step, Uncle Jessie, step, step, Walk, Uncle Jessie, walk, walk, Walk, Uncle Jessie, walk.	Center player takes partner's hands in skating position, and the pair two-step together in the center of the circle.
Now, if you want a sweetheart, I'll tell you what to do, Just take some salt and pepper And sprinkle it in your shoe.	Center players drop hands and stand facing each other, shaking right forefingers at each other. Each center player mimes sprinkling salt in his own right shoe.
Step, Uncle Jessie, step, step, Step, Uncle Jessie, step, etc.	Center players take hands and two-step together as before.
Now if you want Uncle Jessie To do what you want him to do You take some garlic and onion And put it in his shoe.	Center players repeat finger-shaking as before. Center players pretend to put something in their right shoes.
Step, Uncle Jessie, step, step, Step, Uncle Jessie, step, step, Walk, Uncle Jessie, walk, walk, Walk, Uncle Jessie, walk.	Center players take hands and two-step as before. On last word, first center player leaves the center and joins the ring. His partner becomes Uncle Jessie for a repeat of the play.

Uncle Jessie

Way Down Yonder in the Brickyard

And it go on until you get to each one. It's really pretty when you step it together. . . .

In this brief play, dramatic action gives way to a stylized dance step, and the sense of position and pattern begins to dominate over the individual performance of the center player. Because the verse is short, the lead role changes swiftly from person to person. Though clearly a ring play and called so by Mrs. Jones, in action it *feels* like dance. Its simplicity, fast pace, and hot rhythm make it one of the "easiest" plays to learn.

FORM: Ring of players standing and clapping; one player in the center.

LEAD VOICE	GROUP VOICE	ACTION
Way down yonder in the brickyard,	Remember me.	Center player walks around inside ring.
Way down yonder in the brickyard,	Remember me.	Center player stops in front of a ring player and both "step it down" (the *dance* step) four times.
Oh, step it, step it, step it down,	Remember me.	
Oh, swing your love and turn around,	Remember me.	Center player and partner swing halfway around with an elbow swing. This leaves the first player standing as part of the circle; his old partner becomes the new center player for a repeat of the game.

Way Down Yonder in the Brickyard

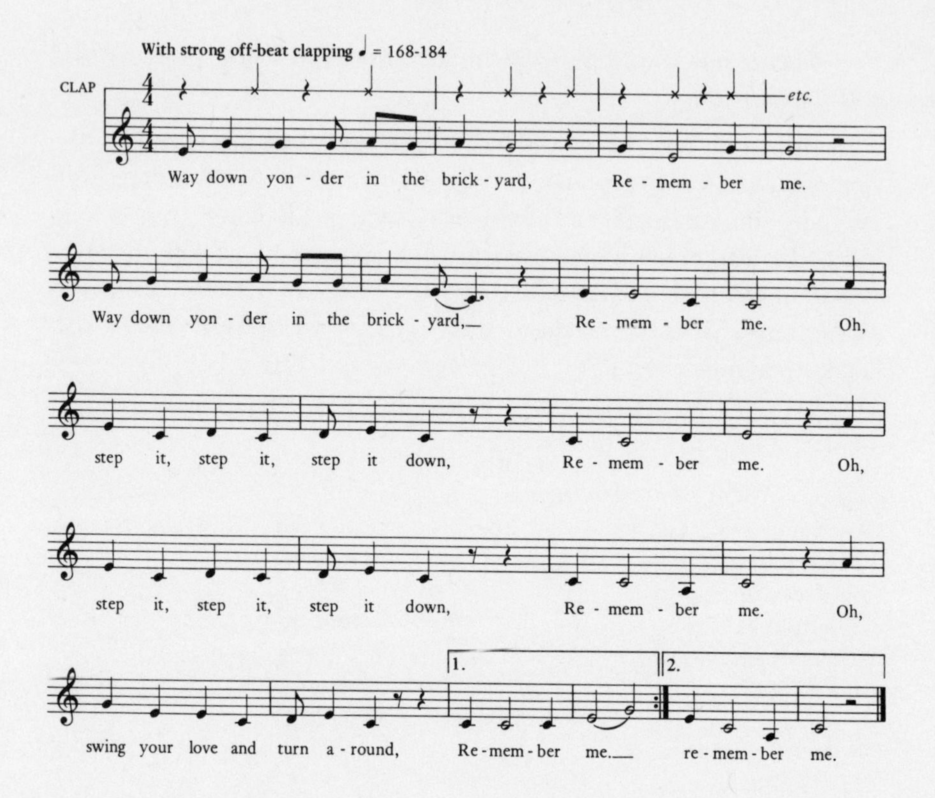

Way Go, Lily

This is just for exercise, to tell the truth; it's just skipping and getting yourself all limbered up. . . .

Besides getting himself "all limbered up," the child dancing the center role in "Way Go, Lily" is released from the circle to find himself truly the ruler at last. Here again is dance developing out of ring play;* instead of acting out a dramatic scene in front of a chosen successor, the center player makes his ruling position clear by swinging each dancer in turn. At the end, as in ring play, he retires to the circle, leaving to another his dancing glory. The joyous and syncopated tune, punctuated by the ominous word "sometimes," should be paced to fit a skipping tempo.

FORM: Circle of children standing and clapping; one center player.

LEAD VOICE	GROUP VOICE	ACTION
Way go, Lily,		Center player skips across the
	Sometimes.	ring and swings any player
Way go, Lily,		once around with an elbow
	Sometimes.	swing. Center player con-
I'm going to rule my ruler,		tinues swinging each child,
	Sometimes.	either in turn or at random
I'm going to rule my ruler,		until all have been swung.
	Sometimes.	She leaves the last dancer in
I'm going to rule him with a hick'ry,		the ring to become the next lead player. The song is re-
	Sometimes.	peated ad lib.
I'm going to rule him with a hick'ry,		
	Sometimes.	

Way go, Lily (2)
I'm going to rule my mother, (2)
I'm going to rule her with a hick'ry. (2)

* This phrase is meant to be understood in a developmental rather than a historical perspective. Mrs. Jones feels that, *in the social growth of the child,* ring play precedes dance; historically, however, it appears that most of her dances are older than most of her ring plays. Further, the oldest of her ring plays, judging by their texts ("Way Go, Lily" and "Uncle Jessie," for example), are also those most closely akin to dance in their patterning and movements. My own explanation of this is that ring play emerged as an important form among Negro children only *after* the Civil War and that it is an outgrowth of and a response to such post-emancipation institutions as segregation laws and the ghetto.

Way go, Lily (2)
I'm going to rule old Master, (2)
I'm going to rule him with a shotgun. (2)

Way go, Lily (2)
I'm going to rule my sister (father, brother, etc.) (2)
I'm going to rule her (him) with a hick'ry. (2)

The song may be sung in stanza form as above, or the lines beginning "I'm going to rule my . . ." may be repeated ad lib as many times as desired.

Way Go, Lily

Steal Up, Young Lady

Didn't you ever play that play they call "Stealing Partners"? . . .

In a further stylization of play into dance, "Steal Up, Young Lady" is a logical follow-up to "Way Go, Lily." Here, one "steals a partner" by dancing out and swinging one member of a couple; the bereft partner then skips off to steal himself a new mate. It's just skipping and swinging and stealing partners, that's all, as Mrs. Jones says.

The two lines

> Steal up, young lady, oh, happy land,
> Won't you steal up, young lady, oh, happy land.

may be considered a chorus and may be repeated after each couplet of the song, or they may be inserted ad lib. The dance step is a skip throughout.

FORM: Circle of children standing in pairs and clapping; one extra player is in the center.

LEAD VOICE	GROUP VOICE	ACTION
Steal up-a, young lady,	Oh, happy land,	Center player skips around in the ring, chooses one
Won't you steal up-a, young lady,	Oh, happy land.	member of a couple whenever he wishes and skips her around with an elbow
If you're going to steal at all,	Oh, happy land,	swing. He has then "stolen" a partner, and the two stand in place, forming a
Steal that man, don't steal no boy,	Oh, happy land.	new couple, while the player who has been left out skips off to continue
Way down yonder where I come from,	Oh, happy land,	the play by "stealing" himself a new partner. Unlike most ring plays, the action
Girls love boys like a hog loves corn,	Oh, happy land.	is not timed to a specific moment in the song, though the rhythm should
Way down yonder in the old cornfield,	Oh, happy land,	be kept, of course. The action is continuous until the players get too tired to
Black snake popped me on my heel,	Oh, happy land.	go on.

I popped my whip, I run
my best,
Oh, happy land,
I run my head in a hornet's
nest,
Oh, happy land.

Steal Up, Young Lady

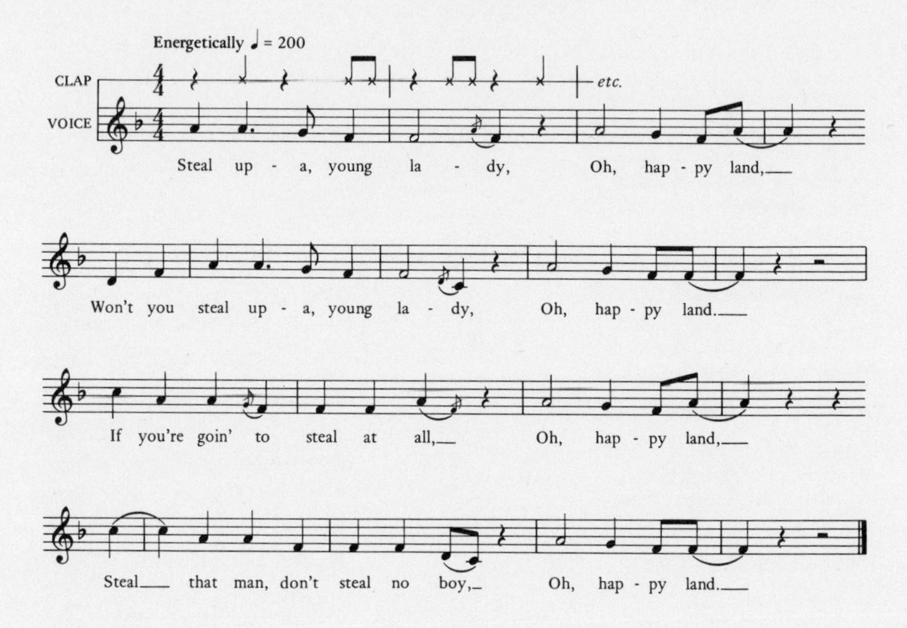

New words and new music adaptation by Bessie Jones; collected and edited with additional new material by Alan Lomax.

6:
Dances

And the other childrens and I would go in the bottom and have a frolic, instead of going to bed. I was just up for that singing, and I remember they used to say, "Come on, Lizzie!"—they called me Lizzie—"Come on, Lizzie!" and we'd go down a way and we'd have a dance.

Oh, it was pretty. . . . You know, it was just as good as the blues—better, better in a way. When the old folks would go to work or go off or something, we'd put on them long dresses and, boy, we'd have a time. I'd be Annie or Elise or somebody—not mocking, but copying, you know—and have a wonderful time. It was fun for the children to do, because there was much joy to it. . . .

Out of the comforting boundaries of the ring, the grown child dances joyfully into the sometimes rigid, sometimes formless patterns of adult life. He uses the same body articulations, the same "steps," but the dramatic content is more abstract, the patterns more varied, the range of personal choice wider. As an adult, he does not "play" any longer; he dances. He has gone through a long apprenticeship; contrary to what the world around him thinks, he is not a "natural" but a thoroughly trained dancer.

If he lives in a Negro rural community, he lives in a world where everybody can dance a little, and almost everybody does, sometime or another. And it is a world where you don't have to go to a special place or wear special clothes or arrange for special music in order to dance. You can dance in the dust of the backyard, on the porch, on a grass patch; you can sing to yourself for an accompaniment, or clap, or tap your heels on the floor. You can dance with the baby or your grandfather or your sister or just all by yourself. Dancing is all mixed in with life, just as work is, or singing.

We'd sing different songs, and then we'd dance a while to rest ourselves. . . .

This relaxed sense of dancing "a while to rest ourselves" may be one reason for the comparative unimportance of *form* in some of Mrs. Jones's dances. After all, if there is no set place in which to dance and no particular number of people dancing, a formal arrangement such as a square or a longways set or even a couple formation may not be practical.

But as I tried to learn such dances as "Sandy Ree" and "Possum Up a 'Simmon Tree," it seemed to me that Mrs. Jones's point of view was almost *too* casual. The plays and games were quite carefully formalized for the most part, but the shape of the dances seemed to melt and shift just when I thought I had finally understood them. "Well, you *could* do it in a circle, or you wouldn't have to if you didn't want to," Mrs. Jones would remark comfortingly, as I tore up one description after another.

The fact is, we were at cross-purposes. I was thinking about form; she was concerned with content. On a more specific level, the *steps* were what she was interested in—not whether the dancers should stand in parallel lines or in a square. She just didn't care where they stood. This does not seem to be simply a peculiarity of Mrs. Jones's; descriptions I have read of Negro dancing during slavery and on through the minstrel-show era cluster around a detailing of the steps, rather than a picture of the dance as a whole. Since this seems to be a historical fact, perhaps history may give some hint as to the cause of it.

Most writers agree that dance was once one of the most highly developed art forms of West Africa (the area from which most Negroes were brought to this country). Dance accompanied and celebrated all human activity; all significant occasions were marked by dance. Transported as slaves to the United States, the new Afro-

Americans were forced to give up their religion, their languages, their customs, their political institutions—all the formal structures that had held their communities together. Like the drums, the old cultural, social, and political instruments had been destroyed.

The impulse to play upon their instruments—to dance—was not. American Negroes continued to dance, continued through their traditional art form to dramatize and celebrate the importance of life. The old organization, however, was no longer possible—the daylong and nightlong festivals, the masks, the complex choreography of a hunting or a fertility ceremonial in which every member of a tribe danced his own appointed role. It seems very possible to me that in the United States, African dance became fragmented in just the same ways in which the old life patterns became fragmented.

There are some exceptions, of course. One of these is religious dance, for the church has been the only institution of any stability in Southern Negro life for generations. (It is no historical accident that Southern churches were the point of organization for integration activity during the 1960's.) Even during slavery Protestant planters did not forbid—and, in many cases, encouraged—religious activity and association in the slave quarters. Since, in Africa, religious celebrations always involve dance, a new kind of holy dance, the "ring shout," was invented by black worshipers in the Southern states, a celebration both of God and of the constancy of the human spirit.

Since the ring shout is not ordinarily danced by children, a full discussion of it is beyond the scope of this book, though I have included one sample, "Daniel," for illustrative purposes. Still, in contrast with our scattered and inconclusive conversations about other kinds of dancing, it was impressive to watch the Islanders organize an old-fashioned ring shout. The circle must move counterclockwise and in single file. The feet must not leave the floor and the legs must not cross; the heels must be kept down. The gestures must follow the vocal directions of the lead singer. The style, the content, and the form were known to all and understood by all. In the only major social institution where some sort of order and continuity were available to the American Negro—the church—there had also developed an orderly and patterned form of dance.

Another area of dance in which form is relatively fixed has already been discussed: children's play, or what might be called "pre-dance."

This is because from the adult point of view the child's world is an ordered one—or it ought to be; and it is important to remember that the plays in this book were taught *by* adults and were thought of as "good for" children. The child's point of view was expressed by Mrs. Jones in one of her reminiscent moods.

In those days they really danced . . . and people played on their guitars, too. We would do it behind mama and them when we were little—all kinds of rawhides and all kinds of twist-es. And we weren't allowed to do twist-es then, you know, but we would do it after they had gone somewhere; we would do it good. . . .

Even as an adult Mrs. Jones remembered how the children wanted to get out of the circle, wanted to learn the grownup "steps."

The last two dances in the section to follow—"Zudie-O" and "I'm Going Away to See Aunt Dinah"—may be examples of a third kind of attempt at stability. There is some evidence that during slavery Negroes adopted by imitation the formal quadrilles danced by their owners in the "big houses," in an effort to become part of the new society into which they had been transplanted. Mrs. Jones recalls that when she was a girl she would shepherd the smaller children away from the grownups to "have our own frolic, and I'd sing and pat and call the sets."

But these are always described as the "old" dances; they are almost, like the ring shout, fading from memory now. Perhaps their shape was wrong; perhaps they dramatized a kind of social order lacking in meaning to American Negroes. The ring play is still alive even in the harsh and sterile streets of the city ghetto; Afro-American versions of the frontier longways set and the square dance live on mainly in a kind of antiquarian atmosphere.

In any event, outside of religious dance, children's play, and the old longways dances, Mrs. Jones's attention to form was perfunctory; the "steps"—the individual statements of condition and emotion—were what she enjoyed. And so such dances as "Sandy Ree," "Ranky Tank," and "Possum Up that 'Simmon Tree" should be approached casually, as she would approach them: "you could do them in a circle, or you wouldn't have to if you didn't want to." Or you don't even have to dance them; just sit and pat and sing.

Possum-La

In 1937 John A. and Alan Lomax recorded for the Library of Congress a little Negro girl from Alabama who sang,

> Put your hands on your hips and let your mind roll forward,
> Back, back, back till you see the stars.
> Skip so lightly, shine so brightly,
> That is the possum-a-la.

The Lomaxes suggest that perhaps she is actually saying "pas-ma-la," a corruption of a French phrase referring to a dance step; this would certainly fit in well with the rest of her song.

Mrs. Jones's version, however, seems clearly focused on a fat possum up in a tree, happily gorging himself and littering the ground below with persimmon seeds. She does know a dance step by the same name as well, and describes it as being "about like the Kneebone Bend." The "Possum-La" dancer shuffles and "cuts up" casually, or perhaps skips around in a circle, until the word "possum-*la*," when he gives a slight jump, or "chug," to one side, landing with his knees deeply bent. The same action is taken on the word "seed." In the refrain, he makes five such jumps, swinging his body from side to side and jumping first at one angle and then at another.

FORM: Indefinite; may be danced alone or in a group. Solo or group singing with patting, heel-tapping, or clapping. Even the song is fluid; this is my own reconstruction of Mrs. Jones's highly varied melody.

Possum up-a that 'simmon tree,
Possum up-a that 'simmon tree,
I don't see nothing but the 'simmon <u>seed</u>.

> Possum-<u>la</u>, possum-<u>la</u>, possum-<u>la</u>, possum-<u>la</u>,
> I don't see nothing but the 'simmon <u>seed</u>.

I want you to catch that possum for me,
I want you to catch that possum for me,
I want you to catch that possum for me,
I don't see nothing but the 'simmon <u>seed</u>.

> Possum-<u>la</u>, possum-<u>la</u>, possum-<u>la</u>, possum-<u>la</u>,
> I don't see nothing but the 'simmon <u>seed</u>.

Possum-la

Highly syncopated; fast, getting faster ♩ = 166-208
Pos - sum up - a that 'sim - mon tree, Pos - sum up - a that 'sim - mon tree, I
don't see noth - ing but the 'sim - mon seed. Pos - sum - la, Pos - sum - la,
Pos - sum - la, Pos - sum - la, I don't see noth - ing but 'sim - mon seed. I
want you to catch that pos - sum for me, I want you to catch that
pos - sum for me, I want you to catch that pos - sum for me, I
don't see noth - ing but the 'sim - mon seed. Pos - sum - la, Pos - sum - la,
Pos - sum - la, Pos - sum - la, I don't see noth - ing but the 'sim - mon seed.

Ranky Tank

This one is good for people on their toes. . . .

The morning Mrs. Jones taught the "Ranky Tank," she also gave a subtle demonstration of how culturally varied the goals of teaching can be. One of the white students was having trouble dancing flat-footed; no matter what the step was, inevitably she would rise up on her toes like a ballerina. The rest of us, all experienced teachers and trying tactfully to be of help, worked out little exercises she could do to force her heels down.

Suddenly Mrs. Jones—equally concerned but operating from a completely different cultural basis—remembered this dance. "This one is *good for* people on their toes!" she announced triumphantly. And so it is, for as she demonstrated it for us, it became clear that people who like to dance on their toes can "Ranky Tank" particularly adeptly.

The Islanders had learned the "Ranky Tank" from the people of nearby Sapelo Island; no one was sure just how the dance was organized, but the chant and step were remembered. The step itself would be called a "buzz" step by dance teachers; the weight is kept on one foot while the other toe pushes the dancer along, very much like the motion of a child riding a scooter. The weighted foot "chugs" along on the downbeat, while the pushing toe touches the floor on the offbeat. The dancer can progress either to the right or to the left (depending on which foot is carrying the weight) and in a straight line or around in a circle.

The "Ranky Tank" chant is improvised, with the various lead lines used as the singer thinks of them. It should be chanted strongly with a pronounced anticipation of the downbeat, and a strong offbeat single or double clap. This is a fine practice piece for dancers learning the buzz step; it's fun just to clap to it, too.

FORM: Indefinite

LEAD VOICE	GROUP VOICE
Oh, ranky tank,	
	Ranky tank.
Oh, ranky tank,	
	Ranky tank.

Papa's goin' to rank,
Ranky tank.
Mama's goin' to rank,
Ranky tank.
Down in the cornfield,
Ranky tank.
I'm goin' to rank,
Ranky tank.
Sun is hot,
Ranky tank.
See me a-rankin',
Ranky tank.
Oh, ranky tank,
Ranky tank.
Oh, ranky tank,
Ranky tank.

Ranky Tank

Coonshine

We thought that was good! We'd just get out in the woods and in the bottom and we'd have a time. . . .

I very much regret that I never saw the "Coonshine" dance; all I have to work from is a tape of Mrs. Jones singing the song. I have decided to include it, however, for its fine tune and the further evidence it shows of the antiquity of Mrs. Jones's tradition.

Almost a hundred years ago, George Washington Cable wrote of seeing the Counjaille dance in New Orleans. According to Harold Courlander, it is still remembered in scattered islands through the West Indies and the term "is still used in southern United States waterfront areas to mean moving or loading cotton, an activity that once, in all probability, was accompanied by Counjaille-type songs and rhythms." Mrs. Jones, whose feelings are really quite mixed on the subject of secular dance, might not have wanted to demonstrate the "Coonshine" for me had I asked her to; judging by the lyrics, in her neighborhood, it was considered a somewhat scandalous performance.

Coonshine, baby, coonshine,
Coonshine on the sly,
Mama don't 'low me to coonshine,
Papa don't 'low me to try,
Onliest way I coonshine,
I coonshine on the sly.

Coonshine, baby, coonshine,
Coonshine, baby, coonshine,
Coonshine, baby, coonshine,
Coonshine on the sly.

Someday I'm goin' coonshine,
Coonshine anyhow,
Mama don't 'low me to coonshine,
Papa don't 'low me to try,
Onliest way I coonshine,
I coonshine on the sly.

Coonshine, baby, coonshine, etc.

When I get grown, I'm goin' coonshine,
Coonshine anyhow,
Mama don't 'low me to coonshine,
Papa don't 'low me to try,
Onliest way I coonshine,
I coonshine on the sly.

Coonshine, baby, coonshine,
Coonshine, baby, coonshine,
Coonshine, baby, coonshine,
Coonshine anyhow!

Coonshine

Stylishly ♩ = 92-112

Coon - shine, ba - by, coon - shine, Coon - shine on the sly,

Ma - ma don't 'low me to coon - shine, Pa - pa don't 'low me to try,

On - li - est way I coon - shine, I coon - shine on the sly.

Coon - shine, ba - by, coon - shine, Coon - shine, ba - by, coon - shine,

Coon - shine, ba - by, coon - shine, Coon - shine on the sly.

Sandy Ree

And in that Sandy Ree, you're doing some pretty dancing. You can turn and swing and have a real party out of it. We just shout and dance to one another, or you can have a regular dance . . . but you do it in front of one another.

It's wonderful to see how the children can carry it. I like that because it ain't dead; it'll never die now, because they got it and gone. . . .

"Sandy Ree" was obviously one of the Islanders' favorite dances; they seemed to reserve their fanciest footwork and their hottest clapping for a "Sandy Ree" session. The word itself may originally have been "sangari," an African term, but the Islanders say that the name comes from the way your feet "scrooch up the sand" when the Sandy Ree step is done.

The step itself is an elaboration of the secular shout step described on page 45. Beginners might do well to practice it in the simplest form first: to an even count of four beats, step right, step left, step right, and "chug" backward on the right foot. Repeat to the other side: step left, right, left, and chug backward on the left foot. This may then be fitted to the song as follows:

	O----O	babe,			Sand----y	ree		
	R	L	R	chug R	L	R	L	chug L
(count)	1	2	3	4	1	2	3	4

This step is used throughout the song, but more experienced dancers may want to elaborate it as the Islanders do. To do the "real" Sandy Ree step, the dancer imagines his feet tracing patterns in the sand. On the count of one, instead of just stepping, put the heel down and dig it in by twisting the foot to the side. Steps on the counts of two and three are unornamented; but on the count of four, while chugging on one foot, swing the other around to the front in a half circle, keeping it "low and draggy to scrape up the sand."

The Islanders usually did this dance in couples, facing and working to one another; sometimes each danced alone, sometimes they held right hands across and pulled each other back and forth in what looked very much like the "jive" dancing style of the 1940's. They told me also of a formal way of dancing the "Sandy Ree," in a longways set, apparently, with head and foot couples who "swing and turn partners and go round," but we could never re-create this version satisfactorily. Probably it was much like "I'm Going Away to See Aunt Dinah."

The song has been as hard to pin down as the dance form; the melody varies greatly from stanza to stanza, and the notes as written here should be taken simply as a point of departure. Be sure to accompany it with a strong clap, and don't be afraid of speeding up; this tune gathers momentum as it goes along. Sometimes the Islanders simply used "Sandy Ree" as a background for a clapping practice, or as a song. Either danced or sung, it was certainly not "dead," and I hope, with Mrs. Jones, that "it'll never die now."

Way down yonder,
Sandy ree,
Where I come from,
Sandy ree,
Girls love boys,
Sandy ree,
Like a hog loves corn,
Sandy ree.

(Refrain, to be used ad lib)
Oh, babe,
Sandy ree,
Oh, babe,
Sandy ree,
Oh, babe,
Sandy ree,
Oh, babe,
Sandy ree.

Papa got the shovel,
Sandy ree (etc.),
Mama got the hoe,
If that ain't farming,
I don't know.

Dog on the porch,
Kicking off fleas,
Chicken in the yard,
Scratching up peas.

Old brother rabbit,
Died with a habit,
In my garden,
Eating up cabbage.

If I live,
To see next fall,
I ain't gonna plant,
No cotton at all.

Mama in the cotton patch,
Picking up cotton,
Papa in town,
Drunk and sloppin'.

Well, if I live,
And I don't get killed,
I'm going back,
To Jacksonville.

Road is wet,
Woods is muddy,
Daddy's so drunk,
He can't stand studdy.

Down in the bottom,
Cotton goes rotten,
Can't get a bale,
It's no need of trottin'.

Your dog bark,
He don't see nothin',
My dog bark,
He done see somethin'.

One of these days,
And it won't be long,
You'll look for me here,
And I'll be gone.

Sandy Ree

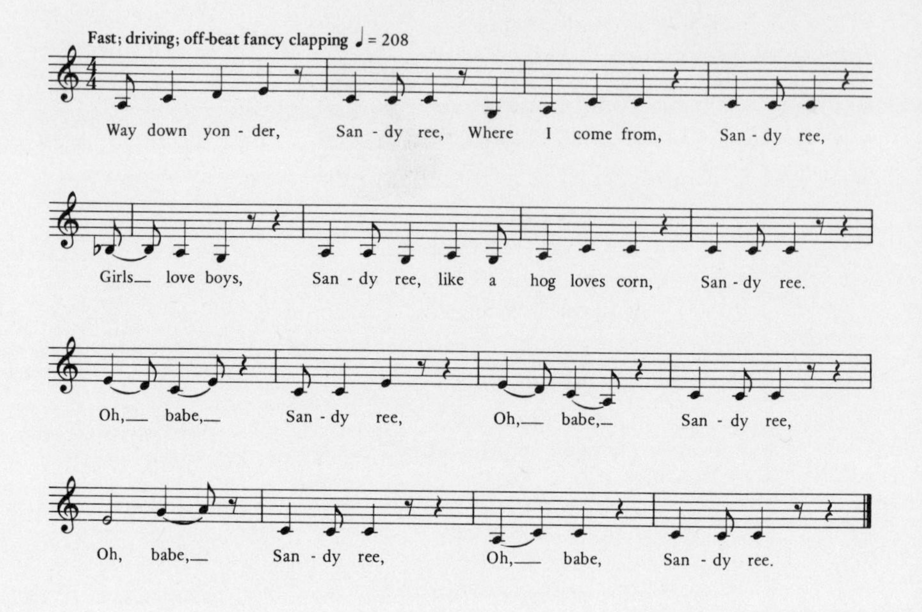
Fast; driving; off-beat fancy clapping ♩ = 208
Way down yon - der, San - dy ree, Where I come from, San - dy ree,
Girls love boys, San - dy ree, like a hog loves corn, San - dy ree.
Oh, babe, San - dy ree, Oh, babe, San - dy ree,
Oh, babe, San - dy ree, Oh, babe, San - dy ree.

Zudie-O

You better say "strutting" instead of "trucking." They're about the same, but the old folks just didn't like you to say it so raw. . . .

The term "zudie-o" refers to a movement in the dance in which the active couple, holding hands in a skating position, pull their arms back and forth alternately in a sawing motion to a count of one, two, three, rest.

Pull	pull	pull	rest	pull	pull	pull	rest
Let's	go	zudie -	o	zudie - o		zudie -	o

Pull	pull	pull	rest	pull	pull	pull	rest
Let's	go	zudie -	o	all	night	long	

The step used in this dance also takes the same count and is a "strutting" two-step: step forward with the right foot, bring the left foot up to a close, step in place with the right foot, and rest. Repeat with the opposite feet.

R L R rest L R
We're walking through the al - ley, al - ley, al - ley,

L rest R L R rest L R L
We're walking through the al - ley, all night long.

"Zudie-O" is still danced by children in big cities across the country, but Mrs. Jones remembers it as a feature of the country dances of her childhood.

It's fun to play it with a big crowd, hear the children hollering way out yonder in the dark about how they want to go zudie-o too. . . . Let's go zudie-o! . . .

ALL VOICES	ACTION
Let's go zudie-o, zudie-o, zudie-o, Let's go zudie-o all night long.	Head lady and gentleman two-step out to meet each other between the lines, take hands, and "go zudie-o" standing still, while the foot couple does the same.
We're walking through the alley, alley, alley, We're walking through the alley all night long.	Head couple two-steps down the inside of the set toward the foot, still holding hands in skating position, while the

	foot couple two-steps similarly up the set.
Step back, Sally, Sally, Sally, Step back Sally, all night long.	Active couples drop hands, face their own partners, and shake right forefingers to the "zudie-o" rhythm. Verses one through three are repeated until the active couples reach the head and foot respectively, where they step back into line.
And here comes another one, 'nother one, 'nother one, Just like the other one all night long. And they're going zudie-o, zudie-o, zudie-o, They're going zudie-o all night long.	The two couples next to the head and foot couples come out and two-step around their partners. The two new active couples take hands and "go zudie-o," and the dance is repeated.

Mrs. Jones says that the final two couples (the ones at the center of the line) can go to the opposite ends instead of just exchanging places with their opposite couples; this allows them more time to "strut" and also reshuffles the order for the next round of dancing.

Zudie-O

Cheerfully; moderate tempo ♩= 144
CLAP
VOICE
etc.
Let's go zu - die - o, zu - die - o, zu - die - o, Let's go
zu - die - o all night long.___ We're walk - ing through the al - ley, al - ley, al -
- ley, We're walk - ing through the al - ley all night long.___ Step back,
Sal - ly, Sal - ly, Sal - ly, Step back Sal - ly, all night long.___
1.
2.
___ And here comes a - noth - er one, 'noth - er one, 'noth - er one, Just like the
oth - er one all night long.___ And they're go - ing zu - die - o, zu - die - o,
zu - die - o, They're go - ing zu - die - o all night long.___

I'm Going Away to See Aunt Dinah

They call it the Virginia Reel now. But we played it when we were little—we didn't know what it was. . . .

This Afro-American version of a frontier dance probably dates back to the time of slavery. It might even be called a museum piece, but one afternoon I saw the Islanders lead off on "I'm Going Away to See Aunt Dinah" with close to one hundred dancers in a mammoth longways set. None of the people dancing that afternoon would label this stirring and syncopated tune "old-fashioned" or "quaint."

As Mrs. Jones points out, "Aunt Dinah" is very much like the Virginia Reel. The step throughout is a skip, and it is danced in two parallel lines, one of men and one of women, facing each other. The lines should be spaced far enough apart to allow each facing couple to skip forward for four beats, swing each other for four and skip back to place for a final count of four. Experienced square dancers may find this "move" of twelve counts against a melody of sixteen to be difficult or jarring. In practice it gives an unexpected syncopation to an otherwise routine figure—a three-against-four count (as in "Juba") in still another form.

The dance is performed as follows:

1. Head and foot couples lead off at the same time and skip down between the parallel lines to meet in a group of four at the center.
2. The head man swings the foot lady with an elbow swing, while the foot man swings the head lady.
3. The head couple continues skipping to the foot to take up new places there; the foot couple in the meantime skips up to the head.
4. The new head man and lady skip toward each other (in four skips) and swing once around with an elbow swing, returning to place.
5. Couple number two then swings in the same manner as the head couple, followed by couple number three, and so on down the line. When the new foot couple has finished its swing, the dance repeats. Unlike the Virginia Reel, the head and foot couples stay the same throughout, simply exchanging places, though the Virginia Reel ending could easily be added.

Unlike those in "Zudie-O," the steps are not timed to any particular words in the accompanying song, which is sung ad lib with a strong lead and sharp clapping. On one occasion I asked Mrs. Jones if I had heard the last couplet correctly—was she really "going away in a coconut shell"? She answered enigmatically, "Yes—that's a *hard* nut."

FORM: Longways set; any number of couples dancing in pattern described above.

LEAD VOICE	GROUP VOICE
I'm goin' away,	
	(To) see Aunt Dinah,
I'm goin' away,	
	(To) see my Lord.

(The above lines serve as a chorus and may be repeated ad lib.)

Bake them biscuits, bake 'em brown,	
	See Aunt Dinah,
Turn them flapjacks around and around,	
	See my Lord.
Preacher come to mama's house,	
	See Aunt Dinah,
Set there and eat till his tongue fall out,	
	See my Lord.
Way down yonder in the old cornfield,	
	See Aunt Dinah,
Black snake popped me on my heel,	
	See my Lord.
I popped my whip, I run my best,	
	See Aunt Dinah,
Run my head in a hornet's nest,	
	See my Lord.
One of these days and it won't be long,	
	See Aunt Dinah,
Look for me and I'll be gone,	
	See my Lord.
Yes, I know something that I ain't going to tell,	See Aunt Dinah,
I'm going away in a coconut shell,	
	See my Lord.

I'm Going Away to See Aunt Dinah

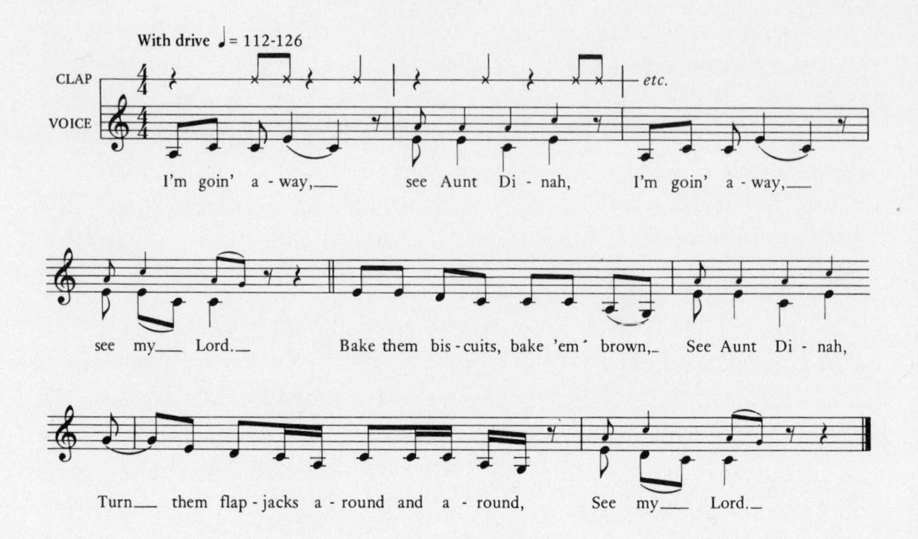

Daniel

No, the ring plays are not exactly like the ring shouts, because you are playing—you see, the children are playing and they mean to play. . . . Some ring plays seem just like a shout in some ways but they are plays. . . . [The children] are not shouting and they better not attempt the shouting in those days, you know what I mean, because the old folks would say you were mocking them and then you'd get a whipping. You see, if you're going to play, you play, and if you're going to shout, you shout. . . .

As Mrs. Jones makes quite clear, the essential distinction between a ring shout and a ring play is the question of fundamental intent. The ring shout is a religious exercise, a form of worship, born out of African tradition and neatly distinguished from secular activities by its purposeful and delimiting structure. It represents a cultural compromise between two groups: Afro-Americans, who felt that it was right and proper to dance before the Lord, and descendants of Calvinism, who regarded any kind of earthbound joys, especially dance, as sinful. The shout, by its emphasis on observance of form and rule, came *outside the concept of dance* for both groups. For example, if you cross your feet or legs, you are no longer shouting but dancing; and, of course, dancing in church would be regarded as an impious activity by *both* white and black worshipers.

The shout "Daniel" is only one of several practiced by the Islanders. It is mimetic in nature; the participants follow the directions of the lead singer. It begins slowly, as the worshipers move into the counterclockwise motion of the circle with slow steps. The phrase "Shout, believer, shout!"—accompanied by the beginning of the stick beating (a broomstick held vertically and pounded on the floor)—comes at a faster tempo and signals the beginning of the shout step, which is then used throughout the ceremonial. The principal rules are these: the circling motion is continuous; the feet leave the floor as little as possible, especial care being taken that the heels stay down; and the legs do not cross—the trailing foot never passes the leading foot. Following are brief descriptions of the specific motions called for:

SHOUT. A rapid shuffling two-step, the back foot closing up to but never passing the leading foot: step (R), close (L); step (R), close (L).

EAGLE WING. Arms bent at elbows are flapped slightly by rotating the shoulder joints in parallel motion. This is the same step as the secular "buzzard lope" move.

ROCK. Bending from side to side at the waist; this movement, like all the others, is restrained.

FLY. Arms stretched out at full length and held stiffly are moved in a sailing motion (if the right arm goes up, the left arm goes down in the same axis). The dancer does not flap; he *soars.*

FLY THE OTHER WAY. Circle reverses movement to clockwise direction; flying motion continues as above.

KNEEBONE BEND. A slight sliding jump landing on both feet with the knees bent sharply; the impact should be timed to the word "bend" (the same step as the secular "Possum-La").

FLY BACK HOME. Fly back in follow-the-leader fashion to your seat; this call signals the end of the shout.

FORM: Circle, clapping if desired; Mrs. Jones occasionally plays tambourine while shouting.* One lead singer, who may dance lead or may beat stick.

LEAD VOICE	GROUP VOICE	ACTION
Walk, believer, walk,†		Circle walks slowly counter-clockwise.
	Daniel,	
Walk, believer, walk,		
	Daniel.	
Walk, I tell you, walk,		
	Daniel,	
Walk, I tell you, walk,		
	Daniel.	
(Tempo almost doubles and stick pounding, if used, begins.)		
Shout, believer, shout,		
	Daniel,	Circle continues in same direction using shout step (which continues throughout).
Shout, believer, shout,		
	Daniel.	
On the eagle wing,		

* As previously mentioned, the term "shout" does not refer to a vocal effect but solely to the dance itself or to the step used in the dance.

† Each phrase sung by the lead singer is repeated four to six times as desired except for the opening phrases, which need only be repeated until the circle is organized.

	Daniel,	Shout step continues; eagle-wing motion is added.
On the eagle wing,		
	Daniel.	
Fly, I tell you, fly,		Shout step continues with flying motion.
	Daniel.	
Rock, I tell you, rock,		Shout step with rocking motion.
	Daniel.	
Fly the other way,		Circle reverses to clockwise direction; shout step and flying motion.
	Daniel.	
Shout, I tell you, shout,		Return to counterclockwise direction; shout step.
	Daniel.	
Give me the kneebone bend,		Shout step continues with a kneebone bend as described.
	Daniel.	
On the eagle wing,		As previously described.
	Daniel.	
Fly, I tell you, fly,		As previously described.
	Daniel.	
Fly back home,		Circle breaks and follows the leader out of the center floor, with shout step and flying motion.
	Daniel.	

Daniel

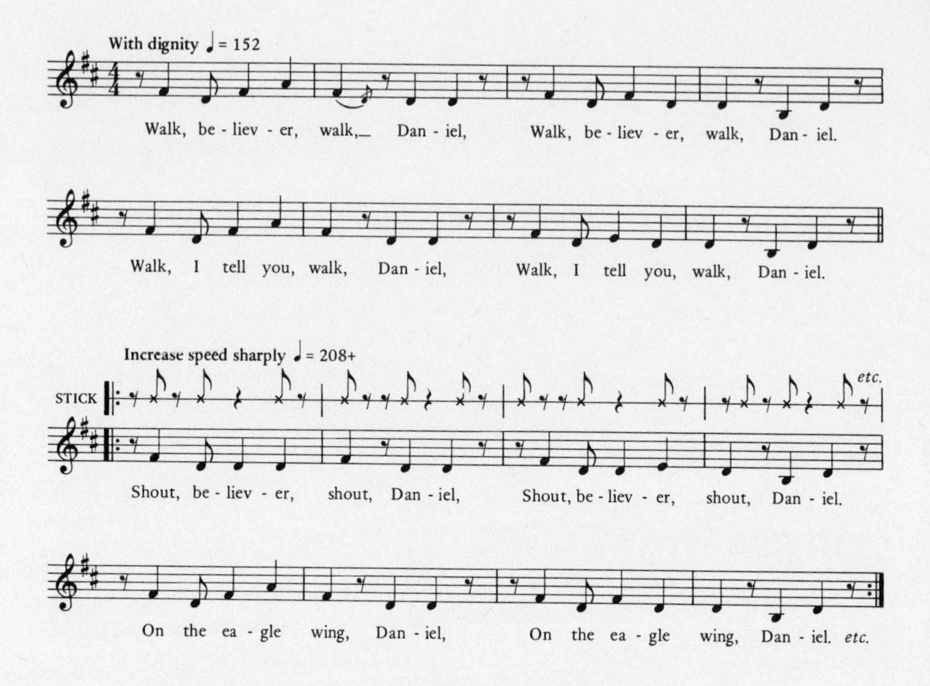
With dignity ♩ = 152
Walk, be - liev - er, walk,— Dan - iel, Walk, be - liev - er, walk, Dan - iel.
Walk, I tell you, walk, Dan - iel, Walk, I tell you, walk, Dan - iel.
Increase speed sharply ♩ = 208+
STICK
etc.
Shout, be - liev - er, shout, Dan - iel, Shout, be - liev - er, shout, Dan - iel.
On the ea - gle wing, Dan - iel, On the ea - gle wing, Dan - iel. etc.

7:
House Plays and Home Amusements

They had happy times . . . they made themselves happy. . . .

Country people have always worked hard. But along with their hard work they have also, as Mrs. Jones puts it, looked for ways to *make* themselves happy.

Big jobs, wherever possible, have been combined with social occasions. Barn-raisings, cornhuskings, and quilting bees suggest the remote and vaguely romantic days of frontier America, but they are within the memory of people now living. Mrs. Jones is one.

I've sit underneath the quilts a many a time threading needles, oh Lord. Fun to me, you know, I'd be alone . . . but like if you were going to have a quilting, other peoples would come to you, and no doubt they'd bring their children and we'd all get underneath the quilt and thread needles and it was fun. . . . We'd eat peanuts, you know, sitting under there and thread needles until we'd get sleepy and they'd have to spread a bed out. . . .

Quilting is not patchwork itself but the act of sewing the completed patched top to its filler and backing with thousands of tiny stitches. Short lengths of thread are used so that the thread may not tangle or knot on itself; eight or ten women sitting around a quilt frame could well use the help of sharp-eyed youngsters as the evening wore on and their own eyes tired.

You be singing hymns and things mostly at quiltings. I never knowed a stitching song yet—you know, a song about stitching. Not me. . . .

Stitching wasn't much to sing about after all; actually songs sung at work rarely talk about the work at hand. From the perspective of the present day, a quilting or a cornhusking sounds like an exciting social affair, but eyes and arms grew tired and backs stiff.

We'd shell peanuts and shuck corn; we'd shell corn, too. We shelled it and then you had to drop it with your hand. I dropped many and many an acre of corn, Lord. And we'd shell the peanuts from house to house, four or five bushels at your house, and we'd tell the crowd, just like a quilting. Friends would gather from one house to another and help shell each farmer's peanuts. And thereby we'd have much fun—stories, you know, and such different things, and songs. . . .

And so they "made themselves happy," throwing all the resources of their imaginations into freeing their spirits from the monotony of their work—and from the monotony of their surroundings, too. For it is worth noting that Mrs. Jones speaks of only one place where the games and dances and parties were held—at home.

During slavery, Negroes were bound to the land they worked; any Negro found on a public road could be questioned and arrested if he could show no written pass. On the plantation itself slaves outside the "quarters" during off hours had to be able to give a good explanation for being found "out of their place." And after emancipation the resources of the black ghettos in both country and town were too meager to support public gathering places—the only exception being the church, tax-free and approved by the white community.

So, except for church meetings and her short schooling, all Mrs. Jones's recollections of happy times are bound into her concept of home—her own house and those of her relatives and friends. From babyhood she had watched the grownups going about their mysterious occupations—working, dancing, talking, singing—all at home, where a little girl could watch. Her poetic temperament and joyful appetite for experience developed in the warm and comfortable places of her childhood—in her own home, around her own house, in her own mother's kitchen.

We would have candy pullings, and you'd catch it and get it started to pull and I'd hand you one end and you hand me the other one and just pull, boy, pull it until it get real shiny—syrup candy, you know. And then you can wring it and you can twist it and plait it, and I've known four to pull at one time; oh, that's pretty, that's pretty that way! And then when you get through and it looks real light tan and pretty, you put it in a big bowl or plate—they had great big platters in those days, big platters, and they would put the candy on there and then you can cut it and eat it for a long time; that candy's there! . . .

Home was where everything happened.

We would have apple-biting parties, either hang 'em on strings or ducking. And we used to have string chewings—that's a nasty job, ain't it? The apple be hanging in the middle and have two people chewing the ends of the string with their hands behind them. The one that chews the most, open his mouth and gets to the apple, that's his apple. Sometimes they get there at the same time—two big mouths on that one apple!—bite it right in two! . . .

Mrs. Jones's parents were farm people, and their friends and neighbors were farmers, too. As their whole life pattern was centered around food getting and food gathering, food was also the central focus of most of their social activities.

We'd have peanut parchings and egg crackings. . . . Egg-cracking parties are good to have now—I'm supposed to have one as soon as I can when I get home. The adults had egg crackings if they were having something for something, like for the church or the school, for you had to buy the books in those days.

They'd boil a lots of eggs and have a party. And different people come and pay—you buy the eggs—in those days, you know, it would be for a nickel or a dime, that was big money; but nowadays it would be twenty-five on up. But you get one egg, and as many eggs as my egg crack, I win those eggs. You're supposed to hit on the end, not on the side, on that sharp end of the egg—not the round end because we know that is easy to break. But we take the two sharp ends, which is hard to break on the egg, and hit them together; and if mine cracks yours, I win your egg. If yours cracks mine, you win mine, and I go and buy another egg. . . .

I'll crack yours and you crack mine,
See whose is thick and whose is fine. . . .

Papa and them learnt to be schemy; they'd boil a rotten egg. You can't break a rotten egg, period, after it's boiled. That rotten egg would win big batches of eggs! . . . That was a dirty papa; he'd hit it right and do it right, but the egg *was crooked! . . . But it wasn't right and they shouldn't have did it, but they did it—it was fun, just win baskets of eggs.*

And you have a wonderful time egg cracking. . . . And we would have candy pullings and peanut parchings, and you can ask riddles at home and you can play ring plays, and you can have different parties, all kinds of parties—so many different things to do. . . .

In the next sections of this book, Mrs. Jones describes some of these "many things to do" that are especially *for* children. She divides them into "outdoor games" and "house plays." Both kinds are fun to play and require little, if any, equipment.

Instead of building blocks, the country child of a generation ago piled up towers of living fists. Instead of using doll houses or puppet theaters, he staged dramatic dialogues with his brothers and sisters. The grownups watched and approved, and probably talked about how, in their day, children didn't have to *play* all the time but knew what real work was.

They had happy times. They *made* themselves happy.

William, William, Trembletoe

He's a rogue—a chicken rogue to catch them hens. He sets up till twelve o'clock and goes to old man Chapman's house to catch chickens. . . .

William, William, Trembletoe
He's a good fisherman to catch them hens,
Put 'em in the pens.
Some lays eggs; some don't.
Wire briar limberlock
Set and sing till twelve o'clock.
The clock fell down,
The mouse ran around.
Y-O-U-T spells Out
To old man Chapman's house.
I went down town the other day
I met my brother Jim. (rest)
He had a hammer, he had a nail,
He had a cat with thirty-nine tails.
Some to the east, some to the west,
Some to the evers goo-goo nest.

Another version of the above rhyme served to count out who would be "it" in the "Hide and Seek" games of my own childhood. Mrs. Jones's version, chanted to a strong rhythm, precedes the playing of a game (essentially a series of conversational scenes) that is known throughout the South. This is how Mrs. Jones describes the playing of it.

You spread your fingers out and count on them; if you got a lot of children, you have just one hand of each child. And then you count on their fingers: "William, William, Trembletoe . . ." The last one when the rhyme ends goes out to the evers goo-goo nest; he goes in a corner. And then the rest of us name ourselves, just whisper to one another names, anything we want to name ourselves—elephant or lion or anything we want to—box, shoe, anything—train, cat—just whatever we surmise to name ourselves. We whisper it [the name chosen] to the one who was counting. And then we have an odd [extra] name, too, that nobody is named. Then you ask the one that's standing out in the corner:

When you coming home?

And he say,

Tomorrow afternoon.

And you say,

What you going to bring?

And he say,

A dish and a spoon and a fat raccoon.

And then we ask him,

What you want to ride on?

And we name all those names and in there we call that odd [extra] name. And he have to say [which he wants to ride on]. If he be unlucky and guess the odd name, he have to come on his tiptoes and not let his heels touch, but if he guesses a name that one of the children has, that child have to go after him. If he's too large for the child to carry, he'd just put his hands on his shoulders and come on in home with him. But if he's a small enough child to tote, he totes him, completely totes him, and bring him on to the one counting. And then the counter says,

What's that you got there?

And the child that's carrying him says,

A bag of nits!

(*That sure sounds rough, but it's a bag of nits.*

And the counter says,)

Shake 'em tell they spit.

And he [the carrier] acts like he's shaking them, and the other one acts like he's spitting. And then the counter asks him [the child being carried],

What would you rather lay on—a thorn bed or a feather bed?

And if he says a feather bed you just turn him loose, you drop him—don't throw him. But if he say a thorn bed, just ease him down very easy, because a feather bed won't hurt but a thorn bed will hurt—you got to squat down and ease him down very easy. . . . Well, you know most children will pick a feather bed rather than a thorn bed and we had much fun playing that way.

Club Fist

Your fist is a club when you ball it up. . . .

This is a game known around the world. In Yugoslavia the dialogue that makes up most of the game ends:

Where are the lords?
They jumped over the fence.
Where is the fence?
The ax cut it down.
Where is the ax?
Death lies there and shows his white teeth.

The Georgia version of this ancient, widespread, and grimly humorous game involves, as Mrs. Jones puts it, "as many [players] as you want only not too many." The first player puts his right fist on the floor or on a table with the thumb sticking up; a second player catches the thumb in his own fist and leaves his own thumb up. As many players (and hands) as are available catch hold similarly, forming a tower of fists piled one on top of the other. The first player asks:

What's that you got there?

The owner of the top fist answers,

Club fist.

The first player asks,

Want me to take it off, knock it off, or pinch it off?

The top player makes his choice and the first player uses his left hand, which he has kept free, to do as requested. The same conversation is repeated with the owner of each fist; when all have been taken, knocked, or pinched off, a dialogue takes place between the second and first player—the second player asking the questions, the first answering.

What you got there?
Cheese and bread.
Where's my cheese?
The rat got it.
Where's the rat?
The cat caught him.

Where's the cat?
The dog killed him.
Where's the dog?
The stick beat him.
Where's the stick?
The fire burned it.
Where's the fire?
The water squenched it.
Where's the water?
The ox drank it.
Where's the ox?
The butcher killed him.
Where's the butcher?
The rope hung him.
Where's the rope?
The knife cut it.
Where's the knife?
The hammer mashed it.
Where's the hammer?
It's buried round the church door, and the first
one I see his teeth, I'm going to give him two
pinches and two hits. . . .

The first player then "cuts the fool" and tries to make the other players laugh—the penalty for "showing his white teeth" being "two pinches and two hits."

Uncle Tom

It's just a house game, you know—a fun game, to play in the house.

Many "fun" games are concerned with attempts to make another player "show his white teeth." But "Uncle Tom," though it somewhat resembles other, better-known games, has a plot line and a bitter hilarity all its own. It is an uproariously funny game while it is being played, but afterward you realize what you've been laughing at. Southern black children did not have to search far for the models they satirized in this game.

Here is Mrs. Jones's description of how it is played:

There's a crowd of children setting round in a place and you get you some little sticks or things and call them nails. You come around to the children and then you knock to this one's door just like you were at the door, you knock. They say,

Who is that?

You say,

Old Man Tom.

They say,

What you want?

You say,

I want to sell some nails. How many pounds you want?

And they'll tell him [Uncle Tom] *one or two pounds or three, and he'll let 'em have one or two or three of those sticks . . . or whatever it is. And then he goes to the next one and say the same way, and they buy the nails and the same thing over. Then he'll go away and stay off a little while—he may change while he's out there, dress all kind of funny ways, you know—put on old crazy ragged clothes or a funny face or old funny hat or anything, you know. Make himself look real ugly and raggedy. Then he'll come back and knock again. They say,*

Who is that?

And he say,

Old Man Tom.

They say,

What you want?

He say,

I want you to pay me for my nails, please.

(*He say it in a funny way, like he was so hongry and tired, you see.*) *And they say,*

I can't pay.

And he say,

You can't pay?

They say,

I can't pay!

He say, like he's crying,

You ain't going to pay Uncle Tom?

And you're not supposed to laugh or not even smile, just be hard *at him, and Uncle Tom have to do all kind of funny things to make you laugh. And if you laugh, then you got to give him the nails back, you see. He got to do all kind of cutting up, dancing and jumping around and making ugly face and all the time asking, "You can't pay? You ain't going to pay Uncle Tom. Poor Uncle Tom, you can't pay?" and all that kind of funny way. And then if he can get you to laugh, he got his nails, and he go to another one and do the same way, with all kind of funny motions.*

It's always who can be so hard, you know, and won't laugh, why he'll be Uncle Tom the next time. . . .

Moneyfoot

Children were honest in those days; they won't do honest now. . . . They ain't no use your trying it [this game] because they ain't going to be honest, and they'll peep and they'll look. . . .

We didn't actually play this game, but it would seem from Mrs. Jones's description that without either a little dishonest peeping or a few broad hints it might go on forever. But I am speaking from the point of view of the middle class, whose houses and lives are choked with material objects. Mrs. Jones's game reflects those times and places in our country where a child could lie on his stomach and list off in a few minutes the things that were in his house. They weren't so very many; he didn't need to peep. And while he was thinking of them, he was a "Moneyfoot."

Here is how Mrs. Jones says you play this game:

The children sit in a circle with their feet stretched out. And the counter points to each foot and says,

> One foot, two foot, three foot Sal,
> Bob demidius English mare,
> Mary, tary, moneyfoot!

And when he says "moneyfoot" and points to that foot, you draw it up and he don't count it no more. He keeps on counting the others. Then, quite natural, when you come to both of your feet being "moneyfoot," then you got no foot to walk on and no foot to count, then you is a moneyfoot.

Then you got to lay down on your stomach, and you close both your eyes and you're not supposed to peep, and the counter holds something over you and says,

> Heavy, heavy, hang over your head.

And the child lying down is supposed to guess what it is. If he guesses wrong (like he guesses it's a bottle and it's glasses) the counter says,

> I'll lay these glasses here until the bottle comes.

The "counter" then lays the wrongly guessed object down by the child on the floor, sometimes on top of him! He finds a new object to be guessed and holds it up saying, "Heavy, heavy, hangs over your head" again.

Sometimes that child will stay there so long you'll get chairs and blankets and everything in the house by him. If he guesses right, he gets up and you start again.

Jack in the Bush

MABEL HILLARY: *The best way to play this is with peanuts or popcorn, and that way whoever wins gets to eat all.*

Two players each have an equal number of counters—popcorn, nuts, stones, etc. One picks up a number of his counters, taking care his opponent does not see how many, and holds them out in his closed fist.

Player 1: Jack in the bush!
Player 2: I'll ride him!
Player 1: How many miles?
Player 2: (Guesses the number of counters.)

If he guesses too many, he must give the first player enough counters to make up the amount guessed. If he guesses too few, the first player must give him the amount lacking. If he guesses right, he wins all the counters in his opponent's fist.

Although Mabel Hillary taught me this game, all the Islanders knew it in varying forms. John Davis had played it:

Jack in the bush!
Cut him down!
How many licks?

In this version, incorrect guesses would be made up with hits. Mrs. Jones had played it as:

Old gray horse!
I'll ride him!
How many miles?

and also

Eggs in the bush!
The old hen lay eggs!
How many eggs?

Mrs. Hillary also remarked that when you played for peanuts, you should say,

Pinochle mine!

Somewhat surprisingly to me, this was the only gambling game the Islanders taught me. Variations of this game have been reported from many parts of the United States and all over Europe. The idea of guessing what is held in a closed fist is ancient indeed; Xenophon reported a method of cheating in such games!

Bob-a-Needle

It's a game. Of course, it's a play, too, but it's a game, a house game. . . . Or either you can play it outdoors.

"Bob-a-Needle" (bobbin needle?) is, for purposes of this game, a pen, a jackknife, or a small stick of wood that can be passed rapidly from hand to hand. All the players but one stand in a tight circle, shoulder to shoulder, holding their hands behind their backs. The extra player stands in the center of the ring; she closes her eyes and holds the bob-a-needle high over her head in one hand. One of the ring players silently creeps up and takes the bob-a-needle from her hand and puts it behind his own back. The center player then opens her eyes and begins singing the lead line of the song; the players in the circle sing the refrain:

LEAD VOICE (AD LIB)	GROUP VOICE
Bob-a-needle,	Bob-a-needle is a-running,
Bob-a-needle,	Bob-a-needle is a-running,
Better run, bob-a-needle,	Bob-a-needle is a-running,
Better hustle, bob-a-needle,	Bob-a-needle is a-running,
I want bob-a-needle,	Bob-a-needle is a-running,
Want to find bob-a-needle,	Bob-a-needle is a-running,
Going to catch bob-a-needle,	Bob-a-needle is a-running,
Turn around, bob-a-needle,	Bob-a-needle is a-running,
Oh bob, bob-a-needle,	Bob-a-needle is a-running.

The lead singer's lines are extemporaneous and can be sung in any order. Mrs. Jones often sang each one twice.

During the singing, the players in the ring pass the bob-a-needle from hand to hand, trying to move as little as possible in order not to make its location obvious. Bob-a-needle may travel clockwise or counterclockwise, and the players may reverse direction at will. The center player meanwhile reaches around the waist and feels the hands of each ring player in turn; she too may go in either direction, but she may not skip players nor run back and forth across the ring. When the center player reverses the direction of *her* search, she must signal this with the lead line, "Turn around, bob-a-needle!"

This game does not end when someone is caught holding the elusive bob-a-needle. Like most of Mrs. Jones's games that involve "losing," the person caught simply pays a forfeit and/or takes over the center role so that the play can begin again. When the players tire, the accumulated forfeits are redeemed by their owners in a new sequence of play. (See "Pawns," page 166.)

Bob-a-Needle

Whose Bag Is My Gold Ring?

After the summer workshop the Islanders and I met for several afternoons of talk and re-recording before they took the long bus ride back home to Georgia. They remembered some new plays then which we didn't have a chance to try out because there weren't enough of us to make the game go. "Whose Bag Is My Gold Ring?" is one that Mrs. Jones remembered after I had asked her to re-record "Bob-a-Needle" so that I was certain I had the tune right. It is a singing game with a pretty tune.

The players stand in a circle and pass a ring or another object from hand to hand. Unlike "Bob-a-Needle," the player in the middle has his eyes shut or is blindfolded, so the object may be passed in front of the players. As the center player feels in each hand, the other children sing,

> Whose bag is my gold ring?
> My gold ring I lost on the train
> When I went to London to marry.

The child who starts the song each time must have the ring, thus cuing the center player to search in the direction from which the solo voice comes.

When the center player finds the ring, a pawn (forfeit) is given up and play continues as in "Bob-a-Needle."

Whose Bag Is My Gold Ring?

Written and adapted by Bessie Jones; collected and edited by Alan Lomax.

Pawns

In such games as "Bob-a-Needle" a player who "loses" does not leave the game, but gives up an article of clothing or some object in his possession to a selected referee, and the play goes on. When the players tire of the first game, the earning back of the "pawns" (the articles given up) forms a kind of coda—a relaxing end play to the game itself. (The Islanders used the term "pawn" for both the forfeited article and the task assigned to redeem it.)

To win back a pawn, a judge and a caller are necessary. The judge sits in a chair; the caller stands behind him and holds a pawned object over his head. The judge should not know what, or whose, the article is.

CALLER: Heavy, heavy, hangs over your head.
JUDGE: Is it ladies' wear or gentlemen's wear?
CALLER: It's [ladies'] wear. What shall be done to the [lady] that owns this wear?

The judge then orders the player in question to perform some action. Some of the "pawns" Mrs. Jones exacted were:

to bark like a dog
to crow like a rooster
to hop like a frog
to say a speech
to sing a song
to wade the green valley (see next play)

Mabel Hillary, of a later generation and "raised up with boys," required more vigorous and difficult pawns:

to stand on your head
to walk on your hands from there to me
to walk like a crab (The player lies down on his back, puts his hands on the floor by his shoulders and pushes up so that his body is held up by his feet and hands. He then "walks," spanking himself on the hips with his hands alternately.)
to walk like a duck (Player squats down, puts his arms around and then between his legs and holds his ankles while "walking.")
to roll the pumpkin (Player sits doubled up with arms wrapped around his knees, holding his ankles tightly with his hands, and rolls all the way over.)

Wade in the Green Valley

The one who is wading the green valley don't say a word; he answers by his feet. . . .

This play is actually a "pawn," a task set a player who wants to win back a forfeited article. The judge may tell him to call out a lady of his choice and "wade the green valley with her."

The gentleman then stands on one side of the room with his lady facing him on the other side. He asks her, "Do you like ——?" (some kind of food, or a person, or a color, or anything he thinks of). If she likes it, she takes one step forward; if she does not like it, she takes one step back. If she is indifferent or undecided, she stands still.

Mrs. Jones continues,

Now when you get close, he says, "Would you like a sweet kiss?" and you got to get that, so that's the last of it. Sometimes they take great big steps, if they like what he calls a lot. . . .

This can be played without being a pawn, Mrs. Jones tells me.

Just line your line of children up and let them wade the green valley—just see what would they say with their feet!

In play, this is extraordinarily dramatic; without music or rhythmic accompaniment, the human body makes its statement.

8:
Outdoor Games

That's a good game; it's good for children . . . makes them strong. . . .

Mrs. Jones, vigorous and active in her sixties, firmly believes that running, pulling, jumping, chasing, and wrestling are important for proper physical development and are therefore "good for children." If her group of "outdoor games" is a small one, it is because she includes in this category only those games which *must* be played outside. Ring games, singing games, and many of the plays included in other sections would normally be played outdoors as well, particularly in the community of overcrowded small farmhouses in which Mrs. Jones grew up.

She has put into this section of games, then, only those big-muscle and rowdy activities which could not possibly be played in the house. And it is in this category, too, that the first real signs of organized competition appear. She seems to approve of competition only when it is socially controlled, as it is in play.

So the children, they don't even know how to play those things now, see. But it's just good fun games, keeps you out of devilment, keeps you from fighting. I never had fights with children when I was little—didn't have time to fight, we had to play. When we wasn't playing, we was eating or sleeping or working—and so that was it. But now they got time to talk about the grown things. . . .

Though it seems unlikely that Mrs. Jones *never* had a fight when she was a child, it is surely true that one of the functions of games is to organize and channel the competitive impulse. Today, Mrs. Jones, like most adults, is firmly on the side of peace and quiet.

Actually, the competitive element, even in her "outdoor games," is very slight indeed. Perhaps little girls in Mrs. Jones's "time coming up" weren't encouraged to play competitive games. Perhaps, as an adult, she has forgotten the rougher pastimes of her childhood—or doesn't choose to recommend them to the next generation. In any event, it is fascinating to see how, throughout the sometimes competitive and always strenuous activities she describes in this chapter, there runs the familiar dramatic impulse—the aesthetic goal of the "beautiful play."

Miss Lucy

We used to stand on the step and see who could jump the further in the yard. . . .

Every adult whose childhood was graced by a home with a front or back porch can remember trying to see who could jump the farthest from the top step. Mrs. Jones says,

We used to sing "Miss Lucy" mostly when we played jumping. We'd put a marker out and everybody stand on the top step and jump the same time.

> Miss Lucy!
> Mama say to send a chew tobacco,
> She'll pay you back tomorrow.
> Hooray! Let's jump!

Horse and the Buggy

The one who can stand the longest, that's all it takes—that can stand the longest without getting drunk and falling over. . . .

Roger Caillois, in his book *Man, Play, and Games,* categorizes one type of play as "the pursuit of vertigo"; "Horse and the Buggy" certainly fits that description. To play it, two children take hands, their arms either crossed or straight, and wheel around, pulling back from each other so that their momentum increases. On the words "way down low," they stoop down, sometimes getting down on their knees, but the whirling motion never stops nor does the direction of spin change.

At this galloping pace, the call-and-response pattern for the singing is an essential.

Horse and the buggy,
    Sail away,
Sail away, horsey,
    Sail away.
Horse and the buggy,
    Sail away,
Sail away, lady,
    Sail away.
Way down low,
    Sail away,
Sail away, lady,
    Sail away.
Horse and the buggy,
    Sail away,
Sail away, horsey,
    Sail away.
Sail away, lady,
    Sail away. . . .

Mabel Hillary, who demonstrated the game with Emma Ramsey, remarked, "When you play it with the boys and they let go your hands, you *would* go sailing . . . sail right on across the yard!"

Horse and the Buggy

Won't You Let the Birdie Out?

Unfortunately I did not see this game being played, as Mrs. Jones only recalled it during a final conversation. From her description, a ring of children stand holding hands tightly while the "birdie" in the center goes around the circle, testing the grip of each pair of hands. Typically, Mrs. Jones acted it out for me in rhythm, pretending to try to break through the hands on the downbeat of each question. She described the lead singer as being the child in the middle, though I imagine he would run out of breath pretty soon, and a member of the ring might well have to take over. The lead should be sung vigorously and ad lib, with any phrases or questions that come to mind, throughout the whole game; the answering chant is crisp. When the birdie finds a weak spot, according to Mrs. Jones, he just *breaks* out.

Is this door locked?
No, child, no.
Is this door locked?
No, child, no.
Won't you let the birdie out?
No, child, no.
Won't you let your birdie out?
No, child, no.
I'll give you a piece of sweet bread.
No, child, no.
I'll give you a piece of biscuit.
No, child, no.

Won't you let your birdie out?
No, child, no. etc.

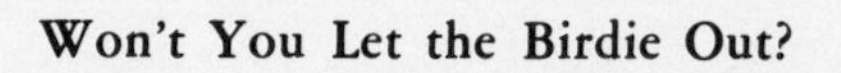
Won't You Let the Birdie Out?

Briskly ♩ = 176
Is this door locked?_ No, child, no. Is this door locked?_
No, child, no. Won't you let the bird - ie out? No, child, no. Won't you
let your bird - ie out?_ No, child, no. I'll give you a piece of sweet bread.
No, child, no. I'll give you a piece of bis - cuit. No, child, no.

Engine Rubber Number Nine

Most of us will recognize this game as the old familiar "Wood Tag," in which an "it" chases the other players, who may find themselves temporary safety by touching wood. As usual with Mrs. Jones's games, the foreplay is more important than the actual game itself.

The children stand in a line with a "caller" facing them. He points to each in turn as he says,

> Engine rubber number nine,
> Stick your head in turpentine.
> Turpentine will make you shine,
> Engine rubber number nine.

Each time the rhyme ends, the child being pointed to comes to the caller. The last one . . .

is Poison and he has to catch the rest of them and poison them. But as long as they're on wood, they're safe—just put their foot on a little chip or anything. And they'll holler out, "I'm free as a jaybird picking up corn!" because they done got on wood, you see, they're free. . . .

Mrs. Jones says you can say this rhyme for a clapping play if you want to, just like "One Saw, Two Saw" or "One-ry, Two-ry." Similarly, either of those rhymes may be used to start off the game just described.

London Bridge

Scholars seem fairly close to agreement that this traditional European game is a reflection of the ancient custom of offering a living sacrifice to the angry spirit of the river when a bridge is to be built. It is among the most widespread of singing games; the Islanders knew two versions.

Mrs. Jones insisted that she sang the tune "just like the children do now." Later, John and Peter Davis sang the tune most usually associated with the game; both their version and Mrs. Jones's included verses that I found unfamiliar.

FORM: Two children hold hands to make an arch through which the other players pass. All sing,

GROUP VOICE	ACTION
London Bridge is all broke down, All broke down, all broke down, London Bridge is all broke down, Pity poor me.	Children walk through the arch in single file, circling around so the line is continuous.
London Bridge is all built up, All built up, all built up, London Bridge is all built up, Pity poor me.	Circling continues as above.
Catch the one that come by last, Come by last, come by last, Catch the one that come by last,	Circling continues.
Pity poor me.	The arched arms come down, catching a player.
Give him a kick and send him home, Send him home, send him home, Give him a kick and send him home, Pity poor me.	The players hold the caught child in the circle of their arms and bump him gently with their knees.

Mrs. Jones continues:

We don't hurt *him, just bump him. . . . Then we* [*the children making the arch*] *done already whispered to one another which one we are, the United States or London. Then we whisper to the child* [*and ask*] *what he'd rather choose, gold or silver. And he got to say;*

then he go behind whichever one. . . . The United States is always silver, you know, and London is gold. . . .

The ones that go behind me, they have to protect me. Then afterwards we go to pulling, you know. And the ones who fall is a rotten egg. And all who's behind me is pulling, and all who's behind you is pulling, you know—a string of them—to see who is the best puller.

Peter and John Davis, Emma Ramsey, and Mabel Hillary sang another version; the play was the same, except that they drew a line under the arch, and during the tug of war, anybody who was pulled over the line had to let go and join the other side. Here is how their song went:

London Bridge is falling down,
Falling down, falling down,
London Bridge is falling down,
Pity poor me.

This is the one that stole my watch,
Stole my watch, stole my watch,
This is the one that stole my watch,
Pity poor me.

Catch that one that come by last,
Come by last, come by last,
Catch that one that come by last,
Pity poor me.

Down to the workhouse he must go,
He must go, he must go,
Down to the workhouse he must go,
Pity poor me.

In the last verse, they may have sung "white house" instead of "workhouse," I am not sure. Since the term "white house" in Negro song generally refers to the plantation mansion, perhaps it doesn't make any difference.

London Bridge

(Mrs. Jones' version)

All Hid

This is another game known all over the world. In country after country, the rules for playing "All Hid" or "Hide and Seek" are remarkably similar; the seeker hides his eyes while the other players scatter; at a certain point, usually determined by counting or reciting a rhyme, the seeker goes out to find the hiders; if successful, he races his quarry back "home." If the hider wins the race, he is "free"; otherwise, he becomes the next seeker. The game is mentioned in more than one of Shakespeare's plays; it is played in India and Rumania and during summer evenings in thc state of Georgia.

Mrs. Jones rightly assumed that everyone knew the "game" part of "All Hid." She was concerned with the dying element of *play*, and her discussion was so eloquent, I include it almost entire, just as she said it.

Children these days don't play like they used to play—nowhere—mine and no one else's. In "Hide and Go Seek," the children nowadays play it right quick and angry—I say angry, because if the one that's counting ask them, "Is all hid?" sometimes they'll holler, "Not yet!" and sometimes they'll just throw off and give a kind of a "No!" and all that way. . . .

But in my time coming up, when the person says, "Is all hid?" he said it in a tone *and the children they answered him in a* tone. *And these tones would combine together, which would make a beautiful play.*

And the children don't count now—well, they really does count—nothing but *counting. They says, "Onetwothreefourfivesixseveneightnineten!" But in those days, we had a* rhyme *that we called counting. Such as, one would go to the base and lean up against a tree and not peeping, because it's not fair, you know, they would hide their eyes and lean against the base and he would say,*

> Honey, honey, bee ball,
> I can't see y'all.
> All hid?

And those children would holler back,

> No-o-o!

And the counter would say,

Is all hid?

And the children would say,

No-o-o!

And sometimes those children be right close to there—but not too close, you know, not too close for the law of the base, ten feet—but they don't be far and they put their hands up to their mouth or put their heads down and say "No-o-o!" real soft. You see, that make him think they're way off! They sound like a panther! . . .

And then it go on like this (singing):

I went to the river,
I couldn't get across,
I paid five dollars for an old blind horse.
One leg broke,
The other leg cracked,
And great Godamighty, how the horse did rack.
Is all hid?
    No-o-o!
Is all hid?
    No-o-o!

I went down the road,
The road was muddy.
Stubbed my toe
And made it bloody.
Is all hid?
    No-o-o!
Is all hid?
    No-o-o!

Me and my wife
And a bobtail dog,
We crossed that river on a hickory log.
She fell in
And I fell off,
It left nobody but the bobtail dog.
Is all hid?
    No-o-o!
Is all hid?
    No-o-o!

One, two,
I don't know what to do.
Three, four,
I don't know where to go.
Five, six,
I'm in a terrible fix.
Seven, eight,
I made a mistake.
Nine, ten,
My eyes open, I'm a-looking!

And they <u>*know*</u> *he's looking. In other words, he could stop right there at "one, two," and when he stop there, they know they better lay close, because he maybe done left the base then because he say, "One, two, I don't know what to do!" He's looking around then, see, let you know he's about to leave the base. "Three, four, I don't know where to go," because they all are hid, see? "Five, six, I'm in a terrible fix"; see, he's looking someplace. "Seven, eight"—he didn't find nobody there—"I made a mistake!"—see? Then he say, "Nine, ten, my eyes* [*are*] *open, I'm a-looking!" and he's going everywhere then, see?*

But the children now don't have that kind of a counting . . . and they won't leave the base! It worries me. I look at them and they won't leave the base, and when the others come, they expect to get their hundred—we called it a "hundred." They call it a base, but in my day, we called it "my hundred." If you make it to the base, if you outrun the counter and get to the base, we called it "my hundred." And you know, when they ask if all is hid, they ask, "All hid?" and they holler back "No!" *and all that. . . . You know, it's no play. It's just a snap all the way through. It's no play in it. . . . But we* played.

All Hid

Steadily ♩ = 120
Hon - ey, hon - ey, bee ball, I can't see y'all. All hid? No - o - o! Is
all hid?__ No - o - o! I went to the riv - er, I
One leg broke, The
could - n't get a - cross, I paid five dol - lars for an old blind__ horse.
oth - er leg cracked, And great God - a - might - y, how the
1.
2.
horse did__ rack.__ Is all hid? No - o - o! Is all__ hid?
No - o - o! I went down the road,__ the road was mud - dy.
Stubbed my toe__ and made it blood - y. All hid? No - o - o! Is
all hid?_ No - o - o! Me and my wife and a bob - tailed dog, We
She fell in and I fell off, It
crossed that riv - er on a hick - 'ry__ log.__
left no - bod - y but the bob - tailed__ dog.__ Is
all hid? No - o - o! Is all hid? No - o - o!
One, two, I don't know what to do. Three, four, I
Five, six, I'm in a ter' - ble fix. Sev - en, eight, I
don't know where to go.
made a mis - take. Nine, ten, My eyes o - pen, I'm a look - ing!

Rap Jack

This grim sport was described by Mrs. Jones in one of her reminiscent moods. I have seen references to a similar "game" called "Wrap Jacket"—a form of duel between boys in the midwest—and also to a like activity engaged in by Arawak Indian boys in Guiana. It is such a formless pursuit as to be exceedingly difficult to trace; I include it here as a reminder of the brutality that lies close to the surface of American history.

Mama and them would take those long switches (and in those days we wore those long dresses and we'd hardly ever see our legs and when we did they wasn't rough and tough like these legs we see now—they was tender—the sun didn't shine on them) and they would play Rap Jack, just hit one another with the switches. I've known them to cut through dresses clean, just cut a tear in them. That's the craziest play to play—I nev-er wanted to play that. . . .

Mama used to play it, too—she was seventeen years old—and they'd stand out there, used to rap jack one another—ooh, the womens and the mens, too. The womens would rap jack the men because you see, the men have on pants. You could get to them closer. . . . I've known them to get those switches and let them sit just to play rap jack. And they'd get hard; that's the reason they'd cut through dresses. The women would cut the men's pants, cut 'em, I tell you. They'd have much fun playing rap jack. . . .

9:
Songs and Stories

I like that. I like that because there's so much <u>*meaning*</u> *to it.*

This final section, unlike the rest of this book, was not really Mrs. Jones's idea, but mine. Furthermore, when it came to choosing the songs and stories to put in, I found I had to do the job myself. She simply did not behave as though there was a separate category of songs and stories *for* children as opposed to those *for* grownups.

There were a few items, such as "Peep Squirrel" or "I Had an Old Rooster," that she identified as "fun for the children," but most of the time she just told stories and sang songs. Anybody might listen and might like them or not. A story would remind her of a riddle and the riddle of a song and the song of another story, just as a conversation drifts from subject to illustration to a complete change of course. And she told or sang whatever came to mind without seeming to worry too much about whether or not it was "suitable" for a particular age group.

This attitude is remarkably different from her feelings about *activities.* To Mrs. Jones, each play and game has its special role in the progressive development of the child. These she had graded and sorted out—but not the verbal material, not the stories and songs. Actually, the plays and games themselves reflect this feeling. Their actions are ordinarily prescribed and fixed; the accompanying songs are wide-ranging in content and often forthrightly adult.

This distinction, it seems to me, further illuminates Mrs. Jones's basic ideas. Motion (dance-play-game) she seems to see as an acting-out, a practicing of the roles and relationships a child must learn. During play, however, the motion is overlain by song; and the song, then, may be a verbal reflection of the kind of a world the child is going to enter. It is never too early for the child to learn what that world is like, and its complexities are suggested by all the subtle devices of poetry.

Now one can see, I believe, a final extension of the principle of antiphony: the constant and continuous interplay of fantasy and reality. The ring player acts out his dream of romantic availability, while the accompanying singers make remarks about how hard it is to find something to eat. As "Lily" dances out her fantasy of domination ("I'm going to rule my ruler!"), the song's chorus both applauds and cautions her—("Sometimes!"). Sometime, someday, the singers tell her, she will have to go outside the ring.

But Lily needs more than a foretaste of the hardness of life; she needs to dream too. Actually, there would be no *play* without both elements. Both the fantasy and the reality are equal in importance.

Perhaps this is why the Singers could still play children's games with delight, though they were all middle-aged or over, and all people of position and dignity in their own community. The adult could be a child, because the child was already adult. Where does one role end and the other begin? Where does the song give over to the dance, the dance to the game, the ruler to the ruled?

The answer suggested by Mrs. Jones's plays seems to me both terribly simple and terribly complex at the same time. They answer each other—the child and the grownup, the hands and the feet, the group voice and the solo voice, the words and the action, the dream world and the real world, in a continual and mutually supportive conversation.

For a conversation implies both mutual respect and mutual need. The feet and the hands are equally important in the clapping pattern. The solo voice cannot function properly without the supporting chorus, and the other way round as well. For Mrs. Jones, there is no dance without song, and no play without "a story to it." And it is out of this mixture, the interweaving of the solid and day-to-day and the fantastic and poetic that the *meaning*, so important to Mrs. Jones, emerges.

And so it would be a serious mistake, I believe, to think about the games and plays in this book just as motion patterns, to dismiss as irrelevant and nonsensical the tangential and luminous language of the songs which surround them. This is why I have added this final section—a sampling of Mrs. Jones's poetry, song, and story—to provide one further glimpse into the life they all express. To quote Mrs. Jones for one final word:

First you say *it (a line from the "Hambone" poem) and then you say it with your* hands *(clapping). It's all the same thing. . . .*

I Had an Old Rooster

Peter [Davis] says he be going out some time he hear one of those birds that holler soon in the morning—maybe it be a jaybird—he say,

Laziness'll kill ya!
Laziness'll kill ya!
Wha!

What the meaning of it is that everything gets up real early in the morning—all but peoples. And those creatures outside would make you know that it's time to get up early in the morning. . . .

All over the world, animals—especially birds—have talked to country people, who have in turn, with their stumbling human tongues, tried to repeat what they have heard. In France, the rooster says "Cocorico!" In England, "Cock-a-doodle-doo!" In Georgia, though, he is more forthright. In a lovely transmutation of sounds, he tells people to get up in the morning and "do early, do early, do."

Mrs. Jones also knows what the jaybirds say, and the owls. Her rooster song goes far back in the Anglo-Irish tradition; her owl story may have been born in the Georgia swamplands. Both themes are centuries old.

I had an old rooster, my rooster pleased me,
I fed my rooster on green berry leaves.
My rooster say cock, cock-a-doodle doodle-doo,
My rooster say do early, do early, do.

I had an old guinea, my guinea pleased me,
I fed my guinea on green berry leaves.
My guinea says pot, pot-a-rack, pot-a-rack,
My guinea says do early, do early, do.

I had an old turkey and my turkey pleased me,
I fed my turkey on green berry leaves.
My turkey says co-look, cook-a-look, cook-a-look,
My turkey says do early, do early, do.

I had an old hen and my hen she pleased me,
I fed my hen on green berry leaves.
My hen say cluck, cluck cluck cluck, cluck cluck,
My hen say do early, do early, do.

(Spoken:) And going on down in there, he did marry a wife, and

I married a wife and my wife pleased me,
I fed my wife just as I pleased.
My wife she grumbled, she grumbled, she grumbled,
My wife she said do early, do early, do.

I Had an Old Rooster

New words and new music adaptation by Bessie Jones; collected and edited with additional new material by Alan Lomax.

Owl Talk

I'll tell you a real story, from my grandfather, about what he did that's real. And I feel so good telling this because it's true. He said so.

He was telling us one time . . . You know my grandfather was a great fisherman, and he would go fishing at night sometimes, come home the next morning, on this great creek called Tanyard Creek. And so he said that . . . late in the afternoon about sundown, he said that the hoot owls—we call them whooping owls because they whoops—they would holler and yell at them [the fishermen] that they may stop fishing so that they could catch their own prey. You see, because the owls fish at night too, you know. And grandpa say that it seem to him like the owl would be talking to him. . . .

Late in the afternoon, he say he would hear the old owl way down the creek . . . getting on about night . . . getting hungry . . . and they fishing . . . and he says one owl would holler down the creek and say, [Mrs. Jones sings in a deep whispery voice]

Fish done or no done,
When night comes, you go home—mmmmmmmmmmah!

He say he hear another old owl, he would holler down the creek and say,

If you can't catch a pike fish
You catch a eel and go home—mmmmmmmmmmmmah!

So one night he say he notice . . . one would holler and then another. And he say, "I want to know what them things are saying! I believe they is talking!"

So one holler across the woods and he say,

Whooo—aaaawww!

And another say,

Ho John!

And John answer, say,

Whooo—aaawww! There's a big dooooo over to my house tonight!

Whooo-aaaall to be there?

And he say,

John the Baptist and his wife and God knows Whooo-aaaall!

Pretty Pear Tree

Throughout children's folklore runs the stream of man's remote past. The young voices and the archaic words contrast strangely but logically, for in country communities the youngest always learn from the oldest—from the grandfathers and grandmothers who have time to sit in the sun and talk and sing with the children.

The cumulative song, with its slow addition and constant repetition, is one of the oldest ways of teaching and remembering. No one has ever traced all the history of "Pretty Pear Tree" (or "The Green Grass Growing All Round," as it is more frequently titled); perhaps it may reach back to man's ancient concerns with springtime and the growth of plants and the eternal mystery of egg and bird.

Mrs. Jones and the Islanders sing this in full barbershop harmony and in the usual cumulative pattern, adding one new element to each repetition until they end with the "hood on the bird and the bird on the egg, the egg in the nest and the nest on the branch, branch on the limb and the limb on the tree and the tree in the ground and the green grass growing all round." With her practical eye on nature, Mrs. Jones says that the "hood on the bird" must mean that the bird is a woodpecker.

Pretty pear tree, pretty pear tree,
Way down yonder.
    Tree in the ground,
    The green grass growing all around and around,
    The green grass growing all around.

And on that tree (and on that tree)
There was a limb (there was a limb),
The prettiest little limb (the prettiest little limb)
I ever did see (I ever did see).
    Limb on the tree and the tree in the ground
    And the green grass growing all around and around,
    The green grass growing all around.

And on that limb (and on that limb)
There was a branch (there was a branch),
The prettiest little branch (the prettiest little branch)
I ever did see (I ever did see).
    Branch on the limb and the limb on the tree,
    Tree in the ground
    And the green grass growing all around and around,
    The green grass growing all round.

And on that branch
There was a nest, etc.

And in that nest
There was an egg, etc.

And on that egg
There was a bird, etc.

And on that bird
There was a head, etc.

And on that head
There was a hood, etc.

Pretty Pear Tree

Riddles

I would like to ask a riddle of you and you can answer me next year when I come back. . . . I'll ask you one now, and if you can answer it now, I'll appreciate it, but if you can't, well, you rhyme it up by next year. Because the way I tell it, you can just see into it and answer it.

A riddle, for Mrs. Jones, is a puzzle, an intellectual exercise, a problem to be studied and pondered over. The style of riddle play popular today, in which the question is asked and immediately answered by the asker, was disappointing and boring to her. However, not having the year she suggested to wait for the answers, I persuaded her and the other Sea Island Singers into a fast exchange of riddling one afternoon:

BESSIE JONES: What is the difference between an egg and a biddy? Twenty-one days. . . . But that's not a riddle; that's a question. . . .

MABEL HILLARY: Well, what's round as a saucer, deep as a cup, And the Pacific Ocean couldn't fill it up? A sifter. . . .
What goes round the house and can't come in?

BESSIE JONES: It come to the door but it won't come in. (It's the same thing.) It's a path . . . a track. . . . That's a clean house, but I've seen some, the track come right on in!

EMMA RAMSEY: What has eyes and cannot see?

BESSIE JONES: A potato.

JOHN DAVIS: Shoes.

EMMA RAMSEY: Naw, it's a needle!

MABEL HILLARY: Well, what in the world is this that goes all around the town, all down town, all across the country and all across the fields, and then come back home (before they quit making them) and sit in the corner with his tongue hanging out? . . . Shoes. But they don't make too many shoes now with tongues in them.

BESSIE JONES: What is this? You ain't got it and you don't want it but if you had it you wouldn't take a thousand dollars for it. You wouldn't take a *million* dollars for it, as far as that's concerned. . . . A bald head. And what is this?

I went down to the whirly wheely whacker
And I met Bum Backer
And I called Tom Tacker
To run Bum Backer
Out of the whirly wheely whacker.

JOHN DAVIS: That's how come I don't go to England. I don't want to mess with that kind of talk. . . .

BESSIE JONES: Now, Tom Tacker is a dog and Bum Backer is a rabbit. Whirly Wheely Whacker is a garden, because, you see, you're in the garden and you're cutting, you see. You whacks and you whirls—you're turning round—you're wheeling and you're whacking. . . .

And what is this?

I went up my ginga gonga,
I come down my winga wonga,
I looked out of my seenfo,
And I see sainfo eating up sanfo.
I called my two little train-and-trickers,
And put em on sainfo,
And made him not eat up sanfo.

Now sanfo is a potato, because they're forced up from the sand. And sainfo, he eating up sanfo. What eats up potatoes raw? Pigs or hogs, that's correct, and he's eating up sanfo. And so I called my two little dogs and put em on the hog to make him not eat up the potatoes. And so it's I went upstairs and come downstairs and looked through my window—that's a seenfo. You see, when you go upstairs, it's a ginga gonga and when you come down, it's a winga wonga because you come *down* faster. . . .

MABEL HILLARY: What is this?

Whitey went in blacky,
Whitey came out of blacky
And left whitey in blacky?

It was a white hen went in a black stump and she laid a white egg and came out and left the egg in the black stump. . . .

And what is this here?

It can constantly move if it choose to, and it have three legs up and ten legs down . . . and there's a human being involved in it?

Well, there's a man with a washpot turned upside down on top of his head, and that's the three legs up. And the man can walk if he choose to or he can stand still; and therefore he got two legs and he got a horse got four legs and a dog named Bob and Bob have four legs. Therefore, he got ten legs down and three legs up.

JOHN DAVIS: Well, if you had a goose and a fox and a sack of corn and you had to carry them across a river and you couldn't carry but one across at a time. . . . Now if you leave the corn with the geese, the geese going to eat it up. If you leave the fox with the goose, he going to eat *him* up. What would you do?

Carry the geese across and you put the geese over there: then you come back and get the corn. You carry the corn over there, and you carry the geese *back. Then* you get the fox and you carry him over, and you come back and get the geese. . . .

MABEL HILLARY: I see a man so ugly he had to slip up on a dipper to get a drink of water and hide behind a washpot for the sun to rise. What's the ugliest you ever see a man?

BESSIE JONES: Those aren't riddles nor either questions. Those are lies.

MABEL HILLARY: Well, the riddles is lies, too.

BESSIE JONES: The riddles is guesswork.

******

I went up the devil's rip rap,
I put up the devil's skip gap.
The devil thought I was so smart
He hitched me to his gocart.
I kicked out from his gocart,
He hitched me to his lead line,
I kicked the devil stone blind.

******

Way Down on the Bingo Farm

The potatoes they grow small because they plant them at the wrong time. You don't plant potatoes in the fall—you dig em. So that's why they eat tops and all, they didn't have anything else to eat. . . .

Mrs. Jones learned this version of a college song from her mother, who had learned it in turn during her school days in rural Georgia. The children marched to it, according to Mrs. Jones's mother. Apparently it must have been the grand march, for

some were turning one way and some the other, and it made a beautiful march. And everyone be on time for the "rig jack jig jack jig" part, and their feet go with the music—"rig jack jig jack jig" [*stop*]. . . .

The phrase "vons of villions" was originally "balm of Gilead," an equally nonsensical expression in this context. Before we had discovered this, Mrs. Jones suggested tentatively that "vons of villions" might be "some kind of a disease that the doctors don't know what else to call it." This would seem to be a most useful term.

There's a girl named Dinah over there,
There's a girl named Dinah over there,
There's a girl named Dinah and her cheeks are made of china.
You can kiss her if you find her over there.

She'll give you vons of villions, vons of villions,
Vons of villions, way down on the Bingo Farm.
And I won't go there any more,
And I won't go there any more,
And I won't go there any more, more, more,
Way down on the Bingo Farm.
And a rig jack jig jack jig,
And a rig jack jig jack jig,
And a rig jack jig jack jig jack jig,
And a rig jack jig jack jig.

Them potatoes they grow small over there,
Them potatoes they grow small over there,
Them potatoes they grow small for they plants them in the fall,
And they eats them tops and all over there.

There is maggots in the cheese over there,
There is maggots in the cheese over there,
There is maggots in the cheese, you can eat them if you please,
You'll get maggots in your teeth over there.

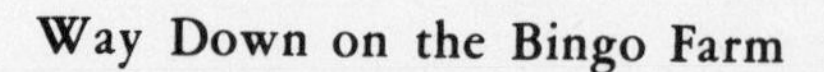

Way Down on the Bingo Farm

Have Courage to Say No

We had schools different to schools now—better than to what I see now. I got a lot of education . . . and the teacher I had, he was a wonderful man, he was really good. They taught you then more Christianity; they taught you good things. And everybody, it looked like, that had understanding, they helped other folks raise their children the right way. Even in school, they help raise children the way they should go. And it wasn't all these juveniles, and all this stuff going on. Although we had mean people ever since the world began, but yet and still the children wasn't that way. The teachers would teach you.

He even taught us about ourselves; he taught the boys and girls how to treat theirselves. He had the big class from the eighth on up to the twelfth, and we'd sit on a different side of the church (we had school in the church) and the little ones on the other side. . . . And he taught the girls how to carry themselves and to keep their bodies clean—the girls especially, because a woman can make a man but very few men can make a woman. A woman when she fall, she's flat as a flounder. You may rise in the sight of God, but people—they'll always have a snare against you. [But] a man can get drunk and [go] naked down the street at night, and tomorrow he's Mister Jack. . . . Well, he taught us these things—how to hold yourself up. . . . And he taught a song to teach boys and girls how to say no. . . .

Have courage, young girls, to say no,
Have courage, young girls, to say no,
Have courage, young girls, have courage, young girls,
Have courage, young girls, to say no.

Have courage, young boys, to say no, etc.

Have courage, old mens, to say no, etc.

And so on. And he would teach us, and then he would teach us the song.

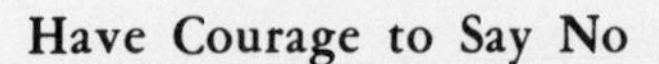

Have Courage to Say No

New words and new music adaptation by Bessie Jones; collected and edited with additional new material by Alan Lomax.

Brother Rabbit and Mister Railroad's Taters

Anyone who loved "Nights with Uncle Remus" as a child or as an adult may find this story vaguely familiar. Actually, it is a retelling of "Brother Fox, Brother Rabbit, and King Deer's Daughter." A point to note is that in both versions the entire plot depends upon the necessity of answering to a call: the principle of antiphony in still another form.

Mrs. Jones told this story with great gusto, pitching her voice up to a thin treble for Brother Rabbit's part of the song, and "bassing" away in a great growl for Brother Wolf.

Brother Rabbit and Brother Wolf were going to see Brother Fox's daughters. Brother Fox had some pretty girls and smart girls . . . oh, and almost everybody called Brother Fox "Mister Railroad," because he was always up and down the railroad tracks stealing chickens.

So, Brother Wolf was very smart and strong and the girls likted him; they would call him to help do different things around the place —that's the story they tell—more than they would Brother Rabbit, because Brother Rabbit's so light and he couldn't do much. Brother Rabbit was light but he liked to do good things and have the girls to call him to help. . . . He got jealous of Brother Wolf.

So, he didn't know any other way to get at Brother Wolf, so he went to Brother Fox's potatoes and he dig up the potatoes in the potato patch—Brother Rabbit did that. He tried to get a trap set for Brother Wolf.

So Brother Fox asked him one day, "Do you know who's going in my potatoes? I want you to watch and help me; somebody's going in my potatoes." (Brother Rabbit says) "I don't know who it is but I sure try to find out."

So, the girls were going to have a big party. Brother Rabbit told Brother Fox, says, "I'll tell you how to do. I found out who's been stealing your taters!" (Taters—they didn't have no potatoes, they had taters in that time.) Brother Fox say, "You did?" Brother Rabbit say, "Yeah, I did!" He say, "I'm going to let him tell you to your face!" Brother Fox say, "Sure enough? You do that for me, I sure be glad; I'll fix him."

All right. Brother Rabbit went on and told Brother Wolf, says, "Brother Wolf, do you know the girls are going to give a party and they want us to play for them? And you've got that big gross voice, you can bass, so I got a little song that we can sing. And when I sing this song, you can bass it, and those girls—oh, those girls be so glad!" Brother Wolf say, "All right!" He's so glad of that, you know, because he want to do everything good for those girls, make 'em happy.

They got right down underneath the hill where nobody couldn't hear them, you know, and Brother Rabbit was teaching him the song. "Now, I'm going to play the guitar and you play the fiddle. When I say,

" 'This is the man that stole Mr. Railroad's taters'

(that was Brother Fox's taters, you know), you must say,

'Yes, my Lord, I am!' "

Brother Wolf say, "All right, how does the song go?" Well, now they begin to stomp:

"This is the man that stole Mr. Railroad's taters!"

(That's Brother Rabbit singing)

"Yes, my Lord, I am, am,

(That's Brother Wolf)

"Yes, my Lord I am!"

Oh, Brother Wolf was just so glad he could bass! Whoo, that was good! And Brother Rabbit just kick up, you know, he was so glad he got him going. They played that for hours under the hill.

They went to the dance that night, setting up there. You know, in that time, in those days, the musicians sets in a corner to themselves, you know. And they sets over there, all tied down, girded down, and they started to play the music. They played other music first, and then they got on to the reel dance for the girls:

This is the man that stole Mr. Railroad's taters!
Yes, my Lord, I am, am,
Yes, my Lord, I am.
This is the man that stole Mr. Railroad's taters!
Yes, my Lord, I am, am,
Yes, my Lord, I am!

And Mr. Railroad stole around there and got Brother Wolf by the collar and jerked him out of there and started beating on him. Brother Wolf asked him, "What's the matter? What I done? What's the matter?" Brother Fox said, "You stole my taters! See, you're the one that's been in my tater patch, eat up my taters." Brother Wolf said, "No, I ain't!" and Brother Fox say, "You just now told me; you told *me you're the one that got it. You told me that to my face!" Brother Wolf say, "Brother Rabbit taught me that song! Brother Rabbit taught me to say that!"*

And then they got out behind Brother Rabbit. . . . You see, that's the time when Brother Rabbit went and told them, he say, "You can do anything you want to do with me, but just don't throw me in the briar patch!" This story run into that one. . . .

Brother Rabbit and Mister Railroad's Taters

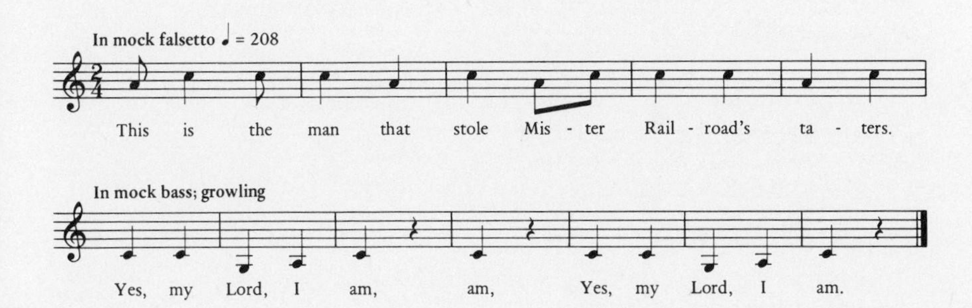

Old Bill the Rolling Pin

When the mule wouldn't do nothing but the possum-la, that means he'd back around and cut up and like that—like he was dancing. . . .

Mrs. Jones says that Old Bill was a "patteroller" and that people made this song up to make fun of him. During slavery, when Negroes were not allowed to leave their home plantations without a pass, "patterollers" were armed guards, hired to patrol the roads at night, enforcing the pass system. This particular "patteroller" had "big eyes and a double chin," apparently reminding the singers of Mister Frog (the same one who went a-courting and who got "struck by a big black snake"). The mule, who dances instead of working, is not as extraneous as he may seem either.

Now, Old Bill the Rolling Pin this morning,
Now, Old Bill the Rolling Pin this morning,
Now, Old Bill the Rolling Pin,
He's up the road and back again,
Big eyes and double chin this morning.

I geed to the mule but the mule wouldn't gee this morning,
I geed to the mule but the mule wouldn't gee this morning,
I geed to the mule but mule wouldn't gee,
I knocked him side the head with the singletree this morning.

Now Old Bill, etc.

I hawed to the mule but the mule wouldn't haw this morning,
I hawed to the mule but the mule wouldn't haw this morning,
I hawed to the mule but the mule wouldn't haw,
He wouldn't do nothing but the possum-la this morning.

Now Old Bill, etc.

Mister Frog went swimming down the lake this morning,
Mister Frog went swimming down the lake this morning,
Mister Frog went swimming down the lake,
But he got swallowed by a big black snake this morning.

Now Old Bill, etc.

(Sung to chorus melody)
Mrs. Duck went swimming down the lake this morning,
Mrs. Duck went swimming down the lake this morning,
Mrs. Duck went swimming down the lake,
But she got struck by a big black snake,
Poor thing, her neck got breaked this morning.

Old Bill the Rolling Pin

Rabbit and the Possum

MRS. JONES: My father used to sing this when I was little childrens. . . . I still sings it to little children—you know, where the rabbit and the possum are going up the hill.

You know, the rabbit's always cunning and sharp and dirty, they say, but he was scared of that possum because he's a big thing and ugly, too. And so they was walking up a hill, as they always walked together in the forest, and so the possum—you know, the possum's got a pocket underneath his stomach—and in that pocket the possum had a forty-dollar bill. (You know there isn't any such thing as a forty-dollar bill.)

So the rabbit, he noticed it, and the rabbit, he didn't know how to get that money. He knew he couldn't take it; he couldn't robber. So they went on up there and the rabbit looked at the possum, say, "Possum, let's play seven-up." The possum say, "All right." They started playing seven-up. They played and played and the rabbit knew he could beat him because he's cunning. He won all Brother Possum's money.

Brother Possum looked at him mean and bad, you know, and kind of grinned, and the rabbit knew good and well he better not bother that money because the possum's going to knock him down. And so that rabbit just got him a *quick* lick, and he knock Brother Possum and Brother Possum fell. (You know the possum will fall stiff every time you hit him.) And the rabbit grabbed that money and over the hill with it and he said, "*Fare* you well!" So that's a song we sing.

> Rabbit and the possum going up the hill,
> Rabbit knowed the possum had a forty-dollar bill.
> Rabbit say, "Possum, let's play seven-up!"
> Rabbit win the money but he's scared to pick it up.
> Rabbit hit the possum, the possum fell,
> Rabbit grab the money, say, "Fare you well!"

A lot of the white childrens like to play that down where I was nursing. I'll play that little song and then I'll make like I'm hitting on 'em, hitting the possum. Then they'll fall just like they're the possum. . . .

MABEL HILLARY: The way I heard it was that the rabbit told the possum that the possum was brown and he was white and they was going to play seven-up, but they weren't going to be like the Negro and the white man. You see, it was the Negro and the white man was playing seven-up, and the Negro won the money and was scared to pick it up.

BESSIE JONES: That little song I know about ain't it hard to be a farmer—that goes in there, too. The colored man win the money but he's scared to pick it up. But we don't say that; we say it's a farmer—it's all the same. . . . It's about it's hard to be a farmer. . . .
(singing)

> Ain't it hard, hard, hard,
> To be a farmer, a farmer, farmer, farmer,
> Ain't it hard, hard, hard,
> You can't get your money when it's due.

> A farmer and a white man was working on a freight,
> Was going out soon but it gets that late.
> White man takes up the farmer's time.
> It always leave poor farmer behind.

> A farmer and a white man was playing seven-up,
> The farmer win the money but he's scared to pick it up.
> The farmer hit the white man, the white man fell,
> The farmer grabbed the money and run like hell.

> The farmer and a white man was walking cross the field,
> Farmer stumbled up on the white man's heel.
> White man cussed and the farmer grinned—
> He knocked that farmer up under his chin.

JOHN DAVIS: Sometimes the white man can't get his money when it's due any more than the farmer. . . .

PETER DAVIS: Mr. Ed Young told me that he ain't never going to eat no more possum because they laugh too much and they ain't nothing funny. . . .

Rabbit and the Possum

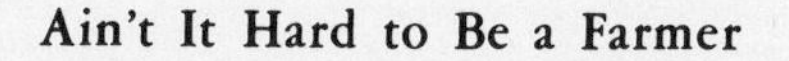

Ain't It Hard to Be a Farmer

Peep, Squirrel

It seems right somehow to bring our book back full circle and end, as we began, with one of Mrs. Jones's songs that she says is especially *for* children. You can sing "Peep, Squirrel" while the children dance, or while you're bouncing a child on your knee; or, at a slower pace, it makes a fine song for a tired baby and a warm lap and a rocking chair. Mrs. Jones says that the "ya di da di deedy um" is the sound of the squirrel's feet scuffling in the leaves, and she sings this song in a somewhat dry and whispery voice and paces it slowly to fit a squeaky chair.

And while she rocks and sings, her fine imaginative mind, nourished by the deep springs of her tradition, sharpened by her sixty years' experience and understanding, ranges slowly over the many surfaces of her little nonsense song.

Peep, squirrel,
  Ya di da di deedy um,
Peep, squirrel,
  Ya di da di deedy um.

Hop, squirrel,
  Ya di da di deedy um,
Hop, squirrel,
  Ya di da di deedy um.

(Each line is repeated as above.)

Run, squirrel,
  Ya di da di deedy um.

Come here, mule,
  Ya di da di deedy um.

Whoa, mule,
  I can't get the saddle on.

Hold that mule,
  I can't get the saddle on.

Go that mule,
  I can't get the saddle on.

Go that squirrel,
  I can't get the saddle on.

Ya di da di deedy um, a
Ya di da di deedy um, dum!

She is searching for *meaning*—for some statement, however fragmentary or slight, about the human condition. "It have to be *about* something." And so, one day, she told me that there was a "story to that song," and, as she told it, the song came alive.

About a little boy in the woods, a little small boy about six years old or better. He seed this squirrel and he couldn't catch the squirrel and he wanted *to catch the squirrel. But the squirrel was too fast for him, playing with him, playing around in the leaves. The squirrel would peep at him and go on up in the tree, you know, and every time the squirrel would go in the leaves, the boy said the leaves would say "ya da deedy um!" (You know—the little feet running in the leaves, "ya da deedy um!" so that's where the "ya di da di deedy um!" come in.)*

He couldn't catch the squirrel and he told him hop, and he'd see the squirrel hop, and he'd run and everything, and he couldn't get that squirrel. And then he see an old mule out there in the pasture not far from there—an old mule walking around, done quit working an' everything, old pet mule. He figured that big old mule could help him get that squirrel, so he call him for help, he call the mule to come here, mule. (The mule didn't know nothing about hunting no squirrel.)

So an old piece of saddle was out there. He picked up the saddle and he gonna do like he seen other people do—throw the saddle on the mule so the mule could help him catch the squirrel. And he couldn't get the saddle up. Every time he tried to throw the saddle, it would hit around the mule's leg; and the mule wouldn't kick him, he'd just kind of walk off from him. The mule didn't want to bother with him; he didn't want to hurt him.

And the squirrel was still running up and down around in the leaves and the tree. So finally, the mule got tired, because he couldn't get the saddle on, and he went to running off, and that scared the squirrel worse, and the squirrel went to running off. So it's "Yonder go that mule!" and "Yonder go that squirrel!" And the boy is standing looking—the mule going one way and the squirrel going the other way—"ya di da di deedy um, ya di da di deedy um dum!" *That's why we wind it up with "dum!" because he couldn't hear it no more. . . .*

So they made a song of it. The song comes after *the story, quite natural, you know, almost always. It have to be* about *something for it to come. . . .*

Peep Squirrel

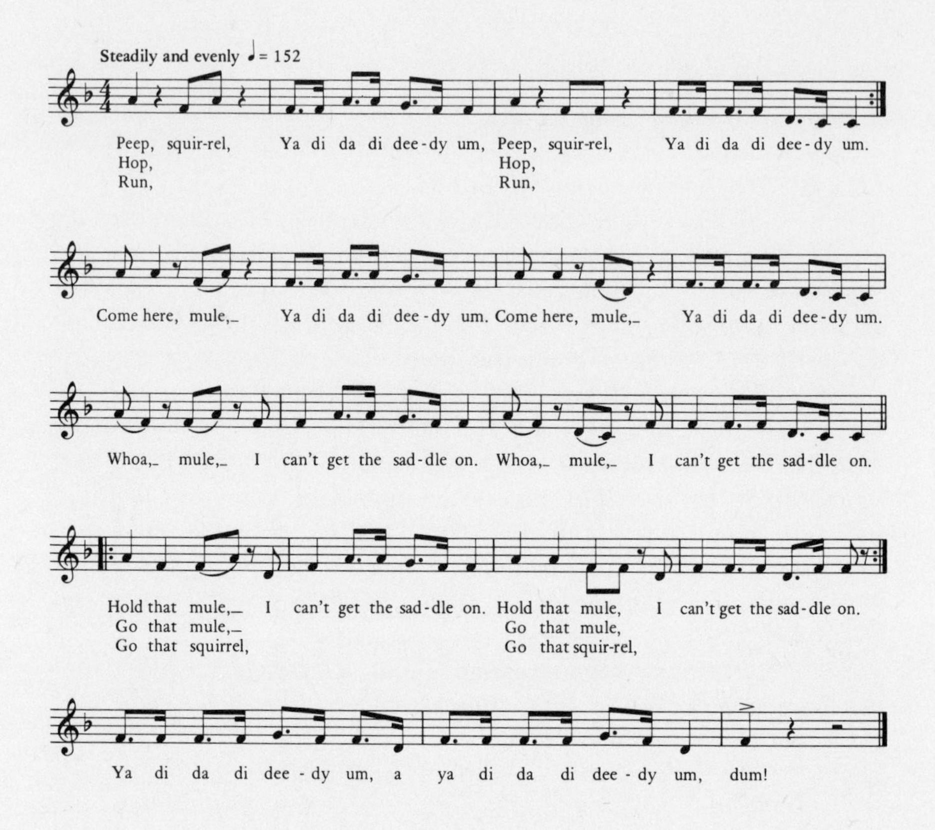

Note to Scholars

1. The work done on this collection was the result of about one month's direct observation of Mrs. Bessie Jones and the Sea Island Singers, as described in the Introduction; during this time, I recorded about forty hours of tapes, including interviews, demonstrations, and teaching sessions. I have further used tapes of interviews loaned to me by Alan Lomax and Ed Cray, as indicated in the acknowledgments.

2. Almost every game has thus been recorded at least twice. I have used and compared all versions; some of the printed texts are portmanteau versions combining several of Mrs. Jones's performances of the same game. Tempo has been recorded, wherever possible, from a tape of the game while it was being performed. Where I have not, for one reason or another, actually seen the game being played, I have mentioned this fact in the head notes.

3. All italicized head notes are direct quotes from taped interviews with Mrs. Jones except where noted. In the case of all but the most generalized observations, these have been remarks made directly about the game being described. I have edited them, in some cases, for comprehensibility; they are essentially verbatim.

4. The musical transcription has been somewhat simplified, due to the impracticality of indicating all of Mrs. Jones's melodic variations. Slides and scoops have been largely eliminated or, where especially important, indicated by grace notes. The original key (usually quite low, because Mrs. Jones's voice is an extraordinarily deep alto) has been raised to a more singable and readable level. Syncopation has been simplified though not eliminated.

5. Unless specified, the entire repertoire may be taken as having come from Mrs. Jones, who seems to have taught the rest of the group. This does not preclude, of course, the possibility that they already knew her version or others. It

has proven impossible, unfortunately, to establish the exact provenience of each item—that is, which come from the mainland and which from St. Simons Island. Mrs. Jones's own memories on exactly where she first heard which song or play were often at sharp variance with those of the other Islanders.

6. Sources consulted for historical data, as well as notations of other published versions (for comparison) have been listed for each song in the section titled "Annotations."

B.L.H.

Annotations

These references in one sense take the place of footnotes; in another, they are designed to aid those who may be interested in investigating individual songs or games more intensively. In the list that follows, where no relevant information or parallel versions have been discovered, the title of the item has simply been omitted.

"Go to Sleepy, Little Baby"
Cf. Brown, vol. 3, pp. 150–53; Lomax (4) pp. 14–15; Scarborough, pp. 145–49; Seeger (1), p. 65; Trent-Johns, pp. 20–21; Work, p. 250.

"This Little Piggy"
Cf. Baring-Gould, pp. 233 and 235; Brown, vol. 1, pp. 185–87; Opie, pp. 348–50; Northall, pp. 416–20.

"Finger Names"
Cf. Baring-Gould, p. 234; Brown, vol. 1, p. 188; Northall, pp. 415–16.

"Patty Cake"
Cf. Abrahams (1), p. 158; Baring-Gould, pp. 239–40; Brown, vol. 1, p. 198; Opie, pp. 341–42; Northall, p. 418.

"Tom, Tom, Greedy-Gut"
Cf. Brown, vol. 1, p. 177; Opie, p. 390; Northall, p. 188.

"Green Sally Up"
Cf. Abrahams (1), p. 72; Brown, vol. 1, p. 172; Talley, p. 116.

"One-ry, Two-ry" and "One Saw, Two Saw"
Cf. Abrahams (1), pp. 146–47; Baring-Gould, pp. 249–50; Bolton, pp. 96–101; Brown, vol. 1, pp. 163–64; Coffin, p. 191; Emrich, p. 100; Jones (for clapping), vol. 1, p. 31; Newell, pp. 197–200; Northall, pps. 344, 348–49; Opie, pp. 335–37.

"Head and Shoulder, Baby"

Cf. Abrahams (2), p. 132.

"Hambone"

Cf. Parrish, pp. 114–16; Scarborough, pp. 46–50; White, p. 218; Talley, pp. 190–95 (rhyme).

"Juba"

Cf. Courlander (1), p. 192; Nathan, pp. 443–46; Parrish, p. 116; Parsons, pp. 199–200; Scarborough, pp. 98–99; White, pp. 161, 163; Talley, pp. 9, 179, 296–97; Turner, p. 101.

"Skip to the Barbershop"

Cf. Durlacher, p. 11; Abrahams (1), p. 65; Emrich, p. 232.

"Just from the Kitchen"

Cf. Courlander (2), p. 67; Parsons, p. 201; Johnson, p. 170.

"Shoo, Turkey"

Cf. Carawan, pp. 132–33; Gomme, pp. 85, 94; Parsons, pp. 200–201; Saxon, p. 446; Talley, pp. 78–79; Johnson, pp. 166–67; Brewer, pp. 371–72; Coffin, pp. 181–82.

"Knock Jim Crow"

Cf. Nathan, pp. 50–52; Opie, pp. 244–45; Scarborough, p. 127; Talley, p. 13; White, pp. 162–63; Lomax (4), p. 78 (for background).

"Josephine"

Cf. Parrish, pp. 106–7; McIntosh, p. 24.

"Elephant Fair"

Cf. Brown, vol. 3, p. 219; Randolph, vol. 3, p. 207; Talley, pp. 159–60.

"Green, Green, the Crab Apple Tree"

Cf. Beckwith, pp. 62–63; Brown, vol. 1, pp. 56–57; Gomme, vol. 1, pp. 170–83; Carawan, p. 129; Newell, p. 71; Northall, p. 362.

"Johnny Cuckoo"

Cf. Botkin, pp. 328–30; Brown, vol. 1, pp. 89–93; Chase, pp. 16–19; Gomme, vol. 2, pp. 233–55; McIntosh, pp. 96–97; Newell, pp. 47–50; Talley, p. 85.

"Oh Green Fields, Roxie"

Cf. Talley, p. 81; Courlander (1), p. 280; (2), p. 69; Newell, p. 56.

"Go In and Out the Window"

Cf. Beckwith, pp. 67–68; Brown, vol. 1, pp. 119–22 and vol. 3, pp. 108–9; Chase, pp. 14–15; Gomme, vol. 2, pp. 122–43; Newell, pp. 128–29; Randolph, pp. 336–38.

"Draw Me a Bucket of Water"

Cf. Baring-Gould, p. 259; Brown, vol. 1, pp. 142–46; Chase, pp. 24–25; Gomme, vol. 1, pp. 100–108; McIntosh, p. 100; Saxon, p. 447; Brewer, pp. 371–72; Northall, pp. 395–96.

"Nana, Thread Needle"

Cf. Beckwith, p. 38; Chase, pp. 30–31; Brewster, pp. 174–75; Gomme, vol. 1, pp. 119, 145–46; vol. 2, pp. 384–87; Parsons, pp. 180, 202; Northall, p. 397.

"Sir Mister Brown"

Cf. Abrahams (1), p. 204; Parsons, p. 178.

"Soup, Soup"

Cf. Saxon, p. 446; Brewer, p. 371; Coffin, p. 183.

"Punchinello"
Cf. Ruth M. Coniston, *Chantons un Peu.* New York, 1929.
"Little Sally Walker"
Cf. Beckwith, pp. 78–79; Brown, vol. 1, pp. 130–31; Courlander (1), pp. 153–54, 275, 278; Courlander (2), p. 75; Gomme, vol. 2, pp. 149–79; Jeckyll, pp. 190–91; Newell, p. 70; Scarborough, p. 142; Trent-Johns, pp. 24–25; Northall, pp. 375–78; Abrahams (1), p. 114; Bolton, p. 120.
"Uncle Jessie"
Cf. Abrahams (2), pp. 129–30; Abrahams (1), p. 62.
"Way Down Yonder in the Brickyard"
Cf. McIntosh, pp. 2–3.
"Way Go, Lily"
Cf. Brewer, p. 370.
"Steal Up, Young Lady"
Cf. Botkin, p. 318; Brown, vol. 1, pp. 101–3, 159; Lomax (2), p. 501; Scarborough, p. 116.
"Possum-La"
Cf. Botkin, pp. 295–96; Brown, vol. 3, pp. 206–7; Jeckyll, p. 214; White, p. 237; Talley, pp. 34–35.
"Ranky Tank"
Cf. Beckwith, p. 61; Carawan, p. 131.
"Coonshine"
Cf. Courlander (1), p. 161; Talley, p. 1; White, pp. 162–63.
"Sandy Ree"
Cf. Courlander (2), pp. 70–71; Parrish, pp. 99–101.
"Zudie-O"
Abrahams (2), pp. 14–17; Trent-Johns, pp. 14–17.
"I'm Going Away to See Aunt Dinah"
Cf. (for verses about blacksnake) White, pp. 245–46.
"Daniel"
Cf. (for background) Courlander (1), pp. 194–200; Lomax (4), p. 335; Turner, p. 202.
"William, William, Trembletoe"
Cf. Beckwith, pp. 12–13; Brewster, pp. 177–78; Brown, vol. 1, pp. 134–37, 160–61; Opie, p. 224; Parsons, p. 203; Johnson, p. 65.
"Club Fist"
Cf. Beckwith, pp. 19–20; Brewster, pp. 30–31; Brown, vol. 1, pp. 66–68; Gomme, pp. 117–19; Newell, pp. 234–35; Johnson, p. 167; Coffin, p. 180.
"Uncle Tom"
Cf. Brewster, p. 23; Northall, pp. 407–8.
"Moneyfoot"
Cf. Beckwith, p. 26; Gomme, vol. 2, pp. 449–50.
"Jack in the Bush"
Cf. Brewster, pp. 8–9; Brown, vol. 1, pp. 60–61; Gomme, vol. 1, pp. 187, 218; Newell, pp. 147–48; Coffin, p. 180.
"Bob-a-Needle"
Cf. Courlander (1), p. 159; Jeckyll, pp. 196–97. Compare "Thimble Game," McIntosh, p. 110.

"Whose Bag Is My Gold Ring"
Cf. Brewster, p. 19; Newell, p. 51.

"Pawns"
Cf. Gomme, vol. 1, p. 143; Newell, p. 143.

"Wade in the Green Valley"
Cf. Brewster, pp. 153–54.

"Horse and the Buggy"
Cf. Brewster, p. 165; Brown, vol. 1, p. 153; McIntosh, p. 24; Newell, p. 170; Talley, p. 20.

"Won't You Let the Birdie Out?"
Cf. Gomme, vol. 1, pp. 50–51, 142–43, 146–47.

"Engine Rubber Number Nine"
Cf. Brewster, pp. 65–66; Brown, vol. 1, pp. 71–74, 168; Gomme, vol. 2, pp. 292–94; Newell, pp. 158–59; Abrahams (1), pp. 48, 184; Emrich, p. 99.

"London Bridge"
Cf. Baring-Gould, pp. 254–57; Brown, vol. 1, pp. 137–40; Gomme, pp. 192–99; Newell, pp. 204–11; Opie, pp. 270–76; Parsons, p. 182; Coffin, p. 176.

"All Hid"
Cf. Brewster, pp. 42–45; Brown, vol. 1, pp. 37–38; Gomme, vol. 1, pp. 211–14; Newell, p. 160; Johnson, p. 166.

"Rap Jack"
Cf. Brown, vol. 1, pp. 157–58; compare "Whipping Toms," Gomme, vol. 1, pp. 217–18.

"I Had an Old Rooster"
Cf. Brown, vol. 3, pp. 172–74; Newell, p. 115; Parsons, p. 184; Talley, p. 145.

"Pretty Pear Tree"
Cf. Brown, vol. 3, pp. 184–85; Newell, pp. 111–13; Randolph, vol. 3, p. 213; Scarborough, p. 359.

"Riddles"
Cf. Scarborough, p. 20; Taylor, p. 35, p. 72 (nos. 199, 200), pp. 152–53 (no. 454), p. 325 (no. 867), p. 649 (no. 1593); Johnson, pp. 156–60; Brewer, pp. 347–52; Coffin, pp. 161, 167, 168; Parsons, pp. 151–175; Emrich, pp. 17, 29, 69.

"Way Down on the Bingo Farm"
Cf. Randolph, vol. 3, p. 384.

"Brother Rabbit and Mister Railroad's Taters"
Cf. Harris, pp. 68–94; Talley, pp. 265–67; Johnson, p. 142.

"Old Bill the Rolling Pin"
Cf. Brown, vol. 3, pp. 154–65; White, pp. 229, 245–46.

"Rabbit and the Possum"
Cf. White, pp. 385–86; Brown, vol. 3, p. 548; Talley, pp. 31–32.

"Peep, Squirrel"
Cf. Botkin, pp. 159–60; Courlander (1), p. 160, and (2), p. 71; Seeger (1), pp. 18–19, 64; Scarborough, pp. 134–36; Talley, p. 78.

Selected Bibliography

An old joke points out that if you steal from one person, it's plagiarism, but if you steal from a hundred, it's original research. I assume the latter activity is what I have been up to, for I find that listing all the books and journals consulted in preparing this manuscript is really impractical. This bibliography, then, contains only those works which I have referred to most frequently and which I would especially like to recommend to the attention of others.

Abrahams, Roger D. ***Jump Rope Rhymes: A Dictionary.*** American Folklore Society Bibliographical and Special Series, Vol. 20. Austin: University of Texas Press, 1969. (1)

Abrahams, Roger D. "There's a Black Girl in the Ring" from ***Two Penny Ballads and Four Dollar Whiskey: A Pennsylvania Folklore Miscellany,*** Kenneth Goldstein and Robert Byington, eds. Hatboro, Pa.: Folklore Associates, 1966. (2)

Baring-Gould, William S. and Ceil. ***The Annotated Mother Goose.*** New York: Clarkson Potter, 1962.

Beckwith, Martha Warren. ***Jamaica Folk-Lore.*** American Folk Lore Society Memoirs, Vol. XXI. New York: G. E. Steckert, 1928.

Bolton, Henry Carrington. ***The Counting-Out Rhymes of Children.*** New York: D. Appleton Co., 1888.

Botkin, Benjamin A. ***The American Play Party Song.*** New York: Frederick Ungar Publishing Co., 1963.

Brewer, J. Mason. ***American Negro Folklore.*** Chicago: Quadrangle Books, 1968.

Brewster, Paul G. ***American Nonsinging Games.*** Norman: University of Oklahoma Press, 1953.

Brown, Frank C. Collection of ***North Carolina Folk Lore.*** Volumes I, III. Newman I. White, ed. Durham, N.C.: Duke University Press, 1952.

Caillois, Roger. ***Man, Play and Games.*** (Paris: 1958). Trans. by Meyer Barash. New York: Glencoe Press, 1961.

Carawan, Guy and Candie. ***Ain't You Got a Right to the Tree of Life,*** New York: Simon and Schuster, 1966.

Chase, Richard. ***Hullabaloo & Other Singing Games.*** Boston: Houghton Mifflin, 1949.

Coffin, Tristram P. and Hennig Cohen. ***Folklore in America.*** New York: Doubleday & Co., 1966.

Courlander, Harold. ***Negro Folk Music U.S.A.*** New York: Columbia University Press, 1963. (1)

———. ***Negro Songs from Alabama.*** New York: Wenner-Gren Foundation, 1960. (2)

Dundes, Alan. "***On Game Morphology: A Study of the Structure of Non-verbal Folklore.***" *New York Folklore Quarterly,* Dec. 1964.

Durlacher, Ed. ***Singing Games for Children.*** New York: Devin-Adair, 1945.

Elder, J. D. ***Song-Games of Trinidad and Tobago.*** Hatboro, Pa.: Folklore Associates, 1965.

Emrich, Duncan. ***The Nonsense Book of Riddles, Rhymes, Tongue Twisters, Puzzles and Jokes from American Folklore.*** New York: Four Winds Press, 1970.

Emrich, Marion Vallat and George Korson. ***The Child's Book of Folklore.*** New York: Dial Press, 1947.

Erikson, Erik F. ***Childhood and Society.*** New York: W. W. Norton (revised 2nd edition), 1963.

Gomme, Alice Mertha. ***The Traditional Games of England, Scotland and Ireland.*** Volumes I and II. (London: 1894 and 1898). New York: Dover reprint, 1964.

Gorer, Geoffrey. ***Africa Dances.*** (London: 1935). New York: W. W. Norton, 1962.

Harris, Joel Chandler. ***Nights With Uncle Remus.*** Boston and New York: D. Appleton Co., 1911.

Herskovitz, Melville. ***The Myth of the Negro Past.*** (New York: 1941). Boston: Beacon Hill Press reprint, 1958.

Hughes, Langston, and Arna Bontemps. ***The Book of Negro Folklore.*** New York: Dodd, Mead & Company, 1958.

Huizinga, Johan. ***Homo Ludens: A Study of the Play Element in Culture.*** (Paris: 1951). Boston: Beacon Hill Press reprint, 1955.

Jeckyll, Walter. ***Jamaican Song and Story.*** (New York: 1907). New York: Dover reprint, 1966.

Johnson, Guy B. ***Folk Culture on St. Helena Island.*** (U. of North Carolina Press: 1930). Hatboro, Pa.: Folklore Associates reprint, 1969.

Jones, A. M. ***Studies in African Music,*** volumes I and II. London: Oxford University Press, 1959.

Lomax, Alan. ***Folksongs of North America.*** New York: Doubleday Doran, 1960. (2)

———. ***Folk Song Style and Culture.*** Washington, D.C.: American Association for the Advancement of Science, 1968. (1)

———. ***The Rainbow Sign.*** New York: Duell Sloan and Pierce, 1959. (3)

Lomax, John A. and Alan. ***Folk Song U.S.A.*** New York: Duell, Sloan and Pearce, 1947. (4)

McIntosh, David S. ***Singing Games and Dances.*** New York: National YMCA Press, 1957.

Muir, Willa. ***Living with Ballads.*** New York: Oxford University Press, 1965.

Nathan, Hans. ***Dan Emmett and the Rise of Early Negro Minstrelsy.*** Norman: University of Oklahoma Press, 1962.

Newell, William Wells. ***Games and Songs of American Children.*** (New York: 1903). New York: Dover reprint, 1963.

Nketia, Kwabena. ***African Music in Ghana.*** Evanston: Northwestern University Press, 1963.

Northall, G. F. ***English Folk Rhymes.*** (London: 1892). Detroit: Singing Tree Press reprint: 1968.

Opie, Iona, and Peter Opie. ***The Oxford Dictionary of Nursery Rhymes.*** London: Oxford University Press, 1961.

Parrish, Lydia E. ***Slave Songs of the Georgia Sea Islands.*** (New York: 1942). Hatboro, Pa.: Folklore Associates reprint, 1965.

Parsons, Elsie Clews. ***Folk-Lore of the Sea Islands, South Carolina.*** Cambridge: American Folk Lore Society Memoirs Vol. XVI, 1923.

Paskman, Dailey, and Sigmund Spaeth. ***Gentlemen, Be Seated.*** New York: Doubleday Doran, 1928.

Randolph, Vance. ***Ozark Folksongs,*** Vol. I, II, III. Columbia, Mo.: State Historical Society of Missouri, 1948.

Saxon, Lyle, Edward Dreyer, and Robert Tallant, eds. ***Gumbo Ya-Ya.*** Boston: Houghton Mifflin, 1945.

Scarborough, Dorothy. ***On the Trail of Negro Folk-Songs.*** (Cambridge: 1925). Hatboro, Pa.: Folklore Associates reprint, 1963.

Seeger, Ruth. ***American Folk Songs for Children.*** New York: Doubleday Doran, 1948. (1)

Seeger, Ruth. ***Animal Folk Songs for Children.*** New York: Doubleday Doran, 1948. (2)

Staff of Music Department, Minneapolis Public Library. ***Index to Folk Dances and Singing Games.*** Chicago: American Library Association, 1936; suppl. 1949.

Sutton-Smith, Brian. ***"Sixty Years of Historical Change in the Game Preferences of American Children."*** *Journal of American Folklore,* 1961.

Talley, Thomas W. ***Negro Folk Rhymes.*** New York: Macmillan, 1922.

Taylor, Archer. ***English Riddles from Oral Tradition.*** Berkeley: University of California Press, 1951.

Trent-Johns, Altona. ***Play Songs of the Deep South.*** Washington, D.C.: Associated Publishers, 1944.

Turner, Lorenzo Dow. ***Africanisms in the Gullah Dialect.*** Chicago: University of Chicago Press, 1949.

Waterman, Richard A. ***"African Influences on the Music of the Americas."*** *Acculturation in the Americas,* Sol Tax, ed. Chicago: University of Chicago Press, 1952.

White, Newman Ivey. ***American Negro Folk Song.*** (Cambridge: 1928). Hatboro, Pa.: Folklore Associates, reprint, 1965.

Work, John W. ***American Negro Songs and Spirituals.*** New York: Bonanza Books, 1940.

Discography

The real musical experience can never be written down. The most detailed notations, the most precise and thorough descriptions, have no "sound." To try to help the reader compensate, I am appending two lists of records. The first contains a listing of commercially available recordings which contain performances, by Mrs. Jones, of some of the material included in this book. The second list includes some recordings containing performances by children of their own traditional games and plays; some are similar to Mrs. Jones's repertoire and some are not. All are worth attention.

Performances by Bessie Jones:

American Folk Songs for Children. Southern Folk Heritage Series. Atlantic 1350.
"Go to Sleep, Little Baby"
"Hambone"
"Johnny Cuckoo"
"Sometimes (Way Down Yonder)"

Deep South—Sacred and Sinful. Southern Journey Series. Prestige/International 25005.
"East Coast Line"

Georgia Sea Islands, Volume II. Southern Journey Series. Prestige/International 25002.
"See Aunt Dinah"

Game performances by children:

Afro-American Blues and Game Songs. Ed. by Alan Lomax. Library of Congress recording AAFS 14.

Been in the Storm So Long. Spirituals, Shouts and Children's Game Songs from Johns Island, South Carolina. Folkways FS 3842.

One Two Three and a Zing Zing Zing. Street games and songs of the children of New York City. Ed. by Tony Schwartz. Folkways FC 7003.

Play and Dance Songs and Tunes. Ed. by B. A. Botkin. Library of Congress recording AAFS L9.

Skip Rope. Thirty-three skip rope games recorded in Evanston, Illinois. Folkways FC 7029.

Index